The Speckled Band by Arthur Conan Doyle

aka The Stonor Case

If ever a writer needed an introduction Arthur Conan Doyle would not be considered that man. After all, Sherlock Holmes is perhaps the foremost literary detective of any age. Add to this canon his stories of science fiction and his poems, his historical novels, his plays, his political campaigning, his efforts in establishing a Court Of Appeal and there is little room for anything else. Except he was also an exceptional writer of short stories of the horrific and macabre. Something very different from what you might expect.

Born in Arthur Conan Doyle was born on 22 May 1859 at 11 Picardy Place, Edinburgh, Scotland. From 1876 - 1881 he studied medicine at the University of Edinburgh following which he was employed as a doctor on the Greenland whaler Hope of Peterhead in 1880 and, after his graduation, as a ship's surgeon on the SS Mayumba during a voyage to the West African coast in 1881. Arriving in Portsmouth in June of that year with less than £10 (£700 today) to his name, he set up a medical practice at 1 Bush Villas in Elm Grove, Southsea. The practice was initially not very successful. While waiting for patients, Conan Doyle again began writing stories and composed his first novel The Mystery of Cloomber. Although he continued to study and practice medicine his career was now firmly set as a writer. And thereafter great works continued to pour out of him.

Index of Contents

HISTORY OF THE PLAY
Dramatisation of the homonymous Sherlock Holmes story
First UK performance: Adelphi Theatre, London, June 4, 1910
First US production: Garrick Theater, New York, November 21, 1910
French's Acting Edition published in 1912

The play (originally title: The Stonor Case) differs from the story in several details, including the names of some of the characters

CAST OF CHARACTERS

MR. SHERLOCK HOLMES— the great detective
MR. SCOTT WILSON— engaged to ENID'S sister
DR. WATSON— Sherlock Holmes' friend
MR. LONGBRACE— Coroner
BILLY— page to SHERLOCK HOLMES
MR. BREWER— foreman of the jury
DR. GRIMESBY RYLOTT— a retired Anglo-Indian Surgeon and owner of Stoke Moran Manor
MR. ARMITAGE— a juror
ENID STONOR— his step-daughter
MR. HOLT LOAMING
ALI— an Indian, valet to DR. RYLOTT
MR. MILVERTON
RODGERS— butler to DR. RYLOTT
MR. JAMES B. MONTAGUE— client of Mr. SHERLOCK HOLMES
MRS. STAUNTON— housekeeper to DR. RYLOTT
CORONER'S OFFICER
INSPECTOR DOWNING

ACT I

The Hall of Stoke Place, Stoke Moran

SCENE. Stoke Place at Stoke Moran. A large, oak-lined, gloomy hall, with everything in disrepair. At the back, centre, is a big double door which leads into the morning-room. To its right, but also facing the audience, is another door which leads to the outside entrance hall. A little down, right, is the door to DR. RYLOTT'S study. Farther down, right, a large opening gives access to the passageway of the bedroom wing. A fifth entrance, up left, leads to the servants' hall. There is a long table in the middle of the room, with chairs round.

ENID STONOR sits on a couch at one side, her face buried in the cushion, sobbing. RODGERS also discovered, the butler, a broken old man. He looks timidly about him and then approaches ENID.

RODGERS - Don't cry, my dear young lady. You're so good and kind to others that it just goes to my heart to see such trouble to you. Things will all change for the better now.

ENID - Thank you, Rodgers, you are very kind.

RODGERS - Life can't be all trouble, Miss Enid. There must surely be some sunshine somewhere, though I've waited a weary time for it.

ENID - Poor old Rodgers!

RODGERS - Yes, it used to be poor young Rodgers, and now it's poor old Rodgers; and there's the story of my life.

(Enter ALI, an Indian servant, from the servants' hall.)

ALI - Mrs. Staunton says you are to have beer and sandwiches for the jury, and tiffin for the coroner.

RODGERS - Very good.

ALI - Go at once.

RODGERS - You mind your own business. You think you are the master.

ALI - I carry the housekeeper's order.

RODGERS - Well, I've got my orders.

ALI - And I see they are done.

RODGERS - You're only the valet, a servant—same as me; as Mrs. Staunton for that matter.

ALI - Shall I tell master? Shall I say you will not take the order?

RODGERS - There, there, I'll do it.

(Enter DR. GRIMESBY RYLOTT from his study.)

RYLOTT - Well, what's the matter? What are you doing Rodgers?

RODGERS - Nothing, sir, nothing.

ALI - I tell him to set out tiffin.

RYLOTT - Go this instant! What do you mean?

(RODGERS exits into servants' hall.)

ALI, stand at the door and show people in. (To ENID.) Oh! for God's sake stop your snivelling! Have I not enough to worry me without that? (Shakes her.) Stop it, I say! I'll have no more. They'll all be in here in a moment.

ENID - Oh? Don't be so harsh with me.

RYLOTT - Hark! I think I hear them. (Crossing toward bedroom passage.) What can they be loitering for? They won't learn much by looking at the body. I suppose that consequential ass of a coroner is giving them a lecture. If Professor Van Donop Doctor WATSON are satisfied, surely that is good enough for him. Ali!

ALI - Yes, Sahib.

RYLOTT - How many witnesses have come?

ALI - Seven, Sahib.

RYLOTT - All in the morning room?

ALI - Yes, Sahib.

RYLOTT - Then put any others in there also.

(ALI salaams.)

Woman will you dry your eyes and try for once to think of other people besides yourself? Learn to stamp down your private emotions. Look at me. I was as fond of your sister Violet as if she had really been my daughter, and yet I face the situation now like a man. Get up and do your duty.

ENID - (drying her eyes) What can I do?

RYLOTT - (sitting on the settee beside her) There's a brave girl. I did not mean to be harsh. Thirty years of India sends a man home with a cayenne pepper temper. Did I ever tell you the funny story of the Indian judge and the cabman?

ENID - Oh, how can you?

RYLOTT - Well, well, I'll tell it some other time. Don't look so shocked. I meant well, I was trying to cheer you up. Now look here, Enid! be a sensible girl and pull yourself together—and I say! be careful what you tell them. We may have had our little disagreements—every family has —but don't wash our linen in public. It is a time to forgive and forget. I always loved Violet in my heart.

ENID - Oh! if I could only think so!

RYLOTT - Since your mother died you have both been to me as my own daughters; in every way the same; mind you say so. D'you hear?

ENID - Yes, I hear.

RYLOTT - Don't forget it. (Rising, turns her face.) Don't forget it. Curse them! are they never coming, the carrion crows! I'll see what they are after.

(Exits into bedroom passage.)

(SCOTT WILSON enters at the hall door and is shown by ALI into the morning-room. While he is showing him in, DR. WATSON enters, and, seeing ENID with her face in the cushions, he comes across to her.)

WATSON - Let me say how sorry I am, Miss Stonor. (Shaking hands.)

ENID - (rises to meet him) I am so glad to see you, Dr. Watson. (Sinks on stool and sobs.) I fear I am a weak, cowardly creature, unfit to meet the shocks of life. It is all like some horrible nightmare.

WATSON - I think you have been splendidly brave. What woman could fail to feel such a shock?

ENID - Your kindness has been the one gleam of light in these dark days. There is such bad feeling between my stepfather and the country doctor that I am sure he would not have come to us. But I remembered the kind letter you wrote when we came home, and I telegraphed on the chance. I could hardly dare hope that you would come from London so promptly.

WATSON - Why, I knew your mother well in India, and I remember you and your poor sister when you were schoolgirls. I was only too glad to be of any use —if indeed I was of any use. Where is your stepfather?

ENID - He has gone in to speak with the coroner.

WATSON - I trust that he does not visit you with any of that violence of which I hear so much in the village. Excuse me if I take a liberty; it is only that I am interested. You are very lonely and defenceless.

ENID - Thank you. I am sure you mean well, but indeed I would rather not discuss this matter.

ALI - (advancing) This way, sir.

WATSON - In a minute.

ALI - Master's orders, sir. (Coming down.)

WATSON - In a minute, I say.

ALI - Very sorry, sir. Must go now.

WATSON - (pushing him away) Stand back, you rascal. I will go in my own time. Don't you dare to interfere with me.

(ALI shrugs shoulders and withdraws.)

Just one last word. It is a true friend who speaks, and you will not resent it. If you should be in any trouble, if anything should come which made you uneasy—which worried you—

ENID - What should come? You frighten me.

WATSON - You have no one in this lonely place to whom you can go. If by chance you should want a friend you will turn to me, will you not?

ENID - How good you are! But you mean more than you say. What is it that you fear?

WATSON - It is a gloomy atmosphere for a young girl. Your stepfather is a strange man. You would come to me, would you not?

ENID - I promise you I will. (Rising.)

WATSON - I can do little enough. But I have a singular friend—a man with strange powers and a very masterful personality. We used to live together, and I came to know him well. Holmes is his name— Mr. Sherlock Holmes. It is to him I should turn if things looked black for you. If any man in England could help it is he.

ENID - But I shall need no help. And yet it is good to think that I am not all alone. Hush! they are coming. Don't delay! Oh! I beg to go.

WATSON - I take your promise with me. (He goes into the morning- room.)

(DR. RYLOTT enters from the bedroom wing, conversing with the CORONER. The JURY,in a confused crowd, come behind. There are a CORONER'S OFFICER and a POLICE INSPECTOR.)

CORONER - Very proper sentiments, sir; very proper sentiments. I can entirely understand your feelings.

RYLOTT - At my age it is a great thing to have a soothing female influence around one. I shall miss it at every turn. She had the sweet temperament of her dear mother. Enid, my dear, have you been introduced to Mr. Longbrace, the Coroner?

CORONER - How do you do, Miss Stonor? You have my sympathy, I am sure. Well, well, we must get to business. Mr. Brewer, I understand that you have been elected as foreman. Is that so, gentlemen?

ALI - Yes, yes.

CORONER - Then perhaps you would sit here. (Looks at watch.) Dear me! it is later than I thought. Now, Dr. Rylott—(sits at table)—both you and your stepdaughter are witnesses in this inquiry, so your presence here is irregular.

RYLOTT - I thought, sir, that under my own roof—

CORONER - Not at all, sir, not at all. The procedure is entirely unaffected by such a consideration.

RYLOTT - I am quite in your hands.

CORONER - Then you will kindly withdraw.

RYLOTT - Come, Enid.

CORONER - Possibly the young lady would wish to be free, so we could take her evidence first.

RYLOTT - That would be most considerate. You can understand, sir, that I would wish her spared in this ordeal. I leave you, dear girl. (Aside.) Remember!

(RYLOTT is about to go into his study but is directed by the INSPECTOR into the morning-room.)

CORONER - Put a chair, there, officer.

(OFFICER places chair.)

CORONER - That will do. Now, Miss Stonor! Thank you. The officer will swear you—

(ENID is sworn by the OFFICER.)

OFFICER – Will tell the truth and nothing but the truth. Thank you.

(ENID kisses the Book.)

CORONER - Now, gentlemen, before I take the evidence, I will remind you of the general circumstances connected with the sudden decease of this unhappy young lady. She was Miss Violet Stonor, the elder of the stepdaughters of Dr. Grimesby Rylott, a retired Anglo-Indian doctor, who has lived for several years at this ancient house of Stoke Place, in Stoke Moran. She was born and educated in India, and her health was never robust. There was, however, no actual physical lesion, nor has any been discovered by the doctors. You have seen the room on the ground floor at the end of this passage, and you realize that the young lady was well guarded, having her sister's bedroom on one side of her and her stepfather's on the other. We will now take the evidence of the sister of the deceased as to what actually occurred. Miss Stonor, do you identify the body of the deceased as that of your sister, Violet Stonor?

ENID - Yes.

CORONER - Might I ask you to tell us what happened upon the night of April 14? I understand that your sister was in her ordinary health when you said good- night to her?

ENID - Yes, she seemed as usual. She was never strong.

CORONER - Had she some mental trouble?

ENID - (hesitating) She was not very happy in her mind.

CORONER - I beg that you will have no reserves. I am sure you appreciate the solemnity of this occasion. Why was your sister unhappy in her mind?

ENID - There were obstacles to her engagement.

CORONER - Yes, yes, I understand that this will be dealt with by another witness. Your sister was unhappy in her mind because she was engaged to be married and there were obstacles. Proceed.

ENID - I was awakened shortly after midnight by a scream. I ran into the passage. As I reached her door I heard a sound like low music, then the key turn in the lock, and she rushed out in her nightdress. Her face was convulsed with terror. She screamed out a few words and fell into my arms, and then slipped down upon the floor. When I tried to raise her I found that she was dead. Then— then I fainted myself, and I knew no more.

CORONER - When you came to yourself—?

ENID - When I came to myself I had been carried by my stepfather and Rodgers, the butler, back to my bed.

CORONER - You mentioned music. What sort of music?

ENID - It was a low, sweet sound.

CORONER - Where did this music come from?

ENID - I could not tell. I may say that once or twice I thought that I heard music at night.

CORONER - You say that your sister screamed out some words. What were the words?

ENID - It was incoherent raving. She was wild with terror.

CORONER - But could you distinguish nothing?

ENID - I heard the word "band"—I also heard the word "speckled." I cannot say more. I was myself almost as terrified as she.

CORONER - Dear me. Band—speckled—it sounds like delirium. She mentioned no name?

ENID - None.

CORONER - What light was in the passage?

ENID - A lamp against the wall.

CORONER - You could distinctly see your sister?

ENID - Oh, yes.

CORONER - And there was at that time no trace of violence upon her?

ENID - No, no!

CORONER - You are quite clear that she unlocked her door before she appeared?

ENID - Yes, I can swear it.

CORONER - And her window? Did she ever sleep with her window open?

ENID - No, it was always fastened at night.

CORONER - Did you examine it after her death?

ENID - I saw it next morning; it was fastened then.

CORONER - One other point, Miss Stonor. You have no reason to believe that your sister contemplated suicide?

ENID - Certainly not.

CORONER - At the same time when a young lady—admittedly of a nervous, highly- strung disposition—is crossed in her love affairs, such a possibility cannot be excluded. You can throw no light upon such a supposition?

ENID - No.

FOREMAN - Don t you think Mr. Coroner if the young lady had designs upon herself she would have stayed in her room and not rushed out into the passage?

CORONER - Well that is for your consideration and judgement. You have heard this young lady's evidence. Have any of you any questions to put?

ARMITAGE - (rising) Well I'm a plain man, a Methodist and the son of a Methodist—

CORONER - What is your name sir?

ARMITAGE - I'm Mr. Armitage sir. I own the big shop in the village.

CORONER - Well sir?

ARMITAGE - I'm a Methodist and the son of a Methodist—

CORONER - Your religious opinions are not under discussion, Mr. Armitage.

ARMITAGE - But I speaks my mind as man to man. I pays my taxes the same as the rest of them.

CORONER - Have you any questions to ask?

ARMITAGE - I would like to ask this young lady whether her stepfather uses her ill for there are some queer stories got about in the village.

CORONER - The question would be out of order. It does not bear upon the death of the deceased.

FOREMAN - Well sir I will put Mr. Armitage's question in another shape. Can you tell us Miss, whether your stepfather ill used the deceased young lady?

ENID - He—he was not always gentle.

ARMITAGE - Does he lay hands on you?—that's what I want to know.

CORONER - Really, Mr. Armitage.

ARMITAGE - Excuse me, Mr. Coroner. I've lived in this village, boy and man for fifty years and I can look any man in the face.

(ARMITAGE sits.)

CORONER - You have heard the question, Miss Stonor. I don't know that we could insist upon your answering it.

ENID - Gentlemen, my stepfather has spent his life in the tropics. It has affected his health. There are times—there are times—when he loses control over his temper. At such times he is liable to be violent. My sister and I thought—hoped—that he was not really responsible for it. He is sorry for it afterwards.

CORONER - Well, Miss Stonor, I am sure I voice the sentiments of the Jury when I express our profound sympathy for the sorrow which has come upon you.

(JURY all murmur, "Certainly," "Quite so," etc.)

Call Mr. Scott Wilson. We need not detain you any longer.

(ENID rises and goes into the morning-room.)

OFFICER - (at door) Mr. Scott Wilson.

(Enter SCOTT WILSON—a commonplace young gentleman.)

CORONER - Swear him, officer—

(SCOTT WILSON mumbles and kisses the Book.)

I understand, Mr. Scott Wilson, that you were engaged to be married to the deceased.

WILSON - Yes, sir.

CORONER - Since how long?

WILSON - Six weeks.

CORONER - Was there any quarrel between you?

WILSON - None.

CORONER - Were you in a position to marry?

WILSON - Yes.

CORONER - Was there any talk of an immediate marriage?

WILSON - Well, sir, we hoped before the summer was over.

CORONER - We hear of obstacles. What were the obstacles?

WILSON - Dr. Rylott. He would not hear of the marriage.

CORONER - Why not?

WILSON - He gave no reason, sir.

CORONER - There was some scandal, was there not?

WILSON - Yes, sir, he assaulted me.

CORONER - What happened?

WILSON - He met me in the village. He was like a raving madman. He struck me several times with his cane, and he set his boar-hound upon me.

CORONER - What did you do?

WILSON - I took refuge in one of the little village shops.

ARMITAGE - (jumping up) I beg your pardon, young gentleman, you took refuge in my shop.

WILSON - Yes, sir, I took refuge in Mr. Armitage's shop.

(ARMITAGE sits.)

CORONER - And a police charge resulted?

WILSON - I withdrew it, sir, out of consideration for my fiancée.

CORONER - But you continued your engagement?

WILSON - I would not be bullied out of that.

CORONER - Quite so. But this opposition, and her fears as to your safety, caused Miss Stonor great anxiety?

WILSON - Yes.

CORONER - Apart from that, you can say nothing which throws any light on this sad event?

WILSON - No. I had not seen her for a week before her death.

CORONER - She never expressed any particular apprehension to you?

WILSON - She was always nervous and unhappy.

CORONER - But nothing definite?

WILSON - No.

CORONER - Any questions, gentlemen. (Pause.) Very good. Call Dr. Watson! You may go.

(SCOTT WILSON goes out through the entrance hall.)

OFFICER - (at morning-room door) Dr. Watson!

(Enter DR. WATSON.)

CORONER - You will kindly take the oath. Gentlemen, at the opening of this Court, and before you viewed the body, you had read to you the evidence of Professor Van Donop, the pathologist who is unable to be present to-day. Dr. Watson's evidence is supplementary to that. You are not in practice, I understand, Dr. Watson?

WATSON - No, sir.

CORONER - A retired Army Surgeon, I understand?

WATSON - Yes.

CORONER - Dear me! you retired young.

WATSON - I was wounded in the Afghan Campaign.

CORONER - I see, I see. You knew Dr. Rylott before this tragedy?

WATSON - No, sir. I knew Mrs. Stonor when she was a widow, and I knew her two daughters. That was in India. I heard of her re-marriage and her death. When I heard that the children, with their stepfather, had come to England, I wrote and reminded them that they had at least one friend.

CORONER - Well, what then?

WATSON - I heard no more until I received a wire from Miss Enid Stonor. I at once came down to Stoke Moran.

CORONER - You were the first medical man to see the body?

WATSON - Dr. Rylott is himself a medical man.

CORONER - Exactly. You were the first independent medical man?

WATSON - Oh, yes, sir.

CORONER - Without going too far into painful details, I take it that you are in agreement with Professor Van Donop's report and analysis?

WATSON - Yes, sir.

CORONER - You found no physical lesion?

WATSON - No.

CORONER - Nothing to account for death?

WATSON - No.

CORONER - No signs of violence?

WATSON - No.

CORONER - Nor of poison?

WATSON - No.

CORONER - Yet there must be a cause?

WATSON - There are many causes of death which leave no sign.

CORONER - For instance—?

WATSON - Well, for instance, the subtler poisons. There are many poisons for which we have no test.

CORONER - No doubt. But you will remember, Dr. Watson, that this young lady died some five or six hours after her last meal. So far as the evidence goes it was only then that she could have taken Poison, unless she took it of her own free will; in which case we Should have expected to find some paper or bottle in her room. But it would indeed be a strange poison which could strike her down so suddenly many hours after it was taken. You perceive difficulty?

WATSON - Yes sir.

CORONER - You could name no such poison?

WATSON - No.

CORONER - Then what remains?

WATSON - There are other causes. One may die of nervous shock or one may die of a broken heart.

CORONER - Had you any reason to think that the deceased had undergone nervous shock?

WATSON - Only the narrative of her sister.

CORONER - You have formed no conjecture as to the nature of the shock?

WATSON - No sir.

CORONER - You spoke of a broken heart. Have you any reason for using such an expression?

WATSON - Only my general impression that she was not happy.

CORONER - I fear we cannot deal with general impressions.

(Murmurs of acquiescence from the JURY.)

You have no definite reason?

WATSON - None that I can put into words.

CORONER - Has any juror any question to ask?

ARMITAGE - (rising) I'm a plain downright man and I want to get to the bottom of this thing.

CORONER - We all share your desire Mr. Armitage.

ARMITAGE - Look here Doctor you examined this lady. Did you find any signs of violence?

WATSON - I have already said I did not.

ARMITAGE - I mean bruises, or the like.

WATSON - No sir.

CORONER - Any questions?

ARMITAGE - I would like to ask the Doctor whether he wrote to these young ladies because he had any reason to think they were ill-used.

WATSON - No, sir. I wrote because I knew their mother.

ARMITAGE - What did their mother die of?

WATSON - I have no idea.

CORONER - Really Mr. Armitage you go too far!

(ARMITAGE sits.)

Anything else?

FOREMAN - May I ask, Dr. Watson, whether you examined the window of the room to see if any one from outside could have molested the lady?

WATSON - The window was bolted.

FOREMAN - Yes, but had it been bolted all night?

WATSON - Yes, it had.

CORONER - How do you know?

WATSON - By the dust on the window-latch.

CORONER - Dear me, Doctor, you are very observant!

WATSON - I have a friend, sir, who trained me in such matters.

CORONER - Well, your evidence seems final on that point. We are all obliged to you, Dr. Watson, and will detain you no longer.

(Exit DR. WATSON into the morning-room.)

OFFICER - (at door) Mr. Rodgers!

(Enter RODGERS.)

CORONER - Swear him!

(Business of swearing.)

Well, Mr. Rodgers, how long have you been in the service of Dr. Rylott?

RODGERS - For many years, sir.

CORONER - Ever since the family settled here?

RODGERS - Yes, sir. I'm an old man, sir, too old to change. I don't suppose I'd get another place if I lost this one. He tells me it would be the gutter or the workhouse.

CORONER - Who tells you?

RODGERS - Him, sir—the master. But I am not saying anything against him, sir. No, no, don't think that—not a word against the master. You won't misunderstand me?

CORONER - You seem nervous?

RODGERS - Well, I'm an old man, sir, and things like this—

CORONER - Quite so, we can understand. Now, Rodgers, upon the night of April 14, you helped to carry the deceased to her room.

RODGERS - Did I, sir? Who said that?

CORONER - We had it in Miss Stonor's evidence. Was it not so?

RODGERS - Yes, yes, if Miss Enid said it. What Miss Enid says is true. And what the master says is true. It's all true.

CORONER - I suppose you came when you heard the scream?

RODGERS - Yes, yes, the scream in the night; I came to it.

CORONER - And what did you see?

RODGERS - I saw—I saw—(Puts his hands up as if about to faint.)

CORONER - Come, come, man, speak out.

RODGERS - I'm—I'm frightened.

CORONER - You have nothing to fear. You are under protection of the law. Who are you afraid of? Your master?

RODGERS - (rising) No, no, gentlemen, don't think that! No, no!

CORONER - Well, then—what did you see?

RODGERS - She was on the ground, sir, and Miss Enid beside her—both in white night clothes. My master was standing near them.

CORONER - Well?

RODGERS - We carried the young lady to her room and laid her on her couch. She never spoke nor moved. I know no more indeed I know no more.

(Sinking into his chair.)

CORONER - Any questions, gentlemen?

ARMITAGE - You live in the house all the time?

RODGERS - Yes, sir.

ARMITAGE - Does your master ever knock you about?

RODGERS - No, sir, no.

ARMITAGE - Well, Mr. Scott Wilson told us what happened to him, and I know he laid the gardener up for a week and paid ten pound to keep out of court. You know that yourself.

RODGERS - No, no, sir, I know nothing of the kind.

ARMITAGE - Well, every one else in the village knows. What I want to ask is —was he ever violent to these young ladies?

FOREMAN - Yes, that's it. Was he violent?

RODGERS - No, not to say violent. No, he's a kind man, the master.

(Pause.)

CORONER - Call Mrs. Staunton, the housekeeper. That will do.

(Exit RODGERS into the servant's hall.)

(Enter MRS. STAUNTON from the morning-room.)

CORONER - You are housekeeper here?

MRS. STAUNTON - Yes, sir. (Standing.)

CORONER - How long have you been here?

MRS. STAUNTON - Ever since the family settled here.

CORONER - Can you tell us anything of this matter?

MRS. STAUNTON - I knew nothing of it, sir, till after the poor young lady had been laid upon the bed. After that it was I who took charge of things, for Dr. Rylott was so dreadfully upset that he could do nothing.

CORONER - Oh! he was very upset, was he?

MRS. STAUNTON - I never saw a man in such a state of grief.

CORONER - Living in the house you had numerous opportunities of seeing the relations between Dr. Rylott and his two stepdaughters.

MRS. STAUNTON - Yes, sir.

CORONER - How would you describe them?

MRS. STAUNTON - He was kindness itself to them. No two young ladies could be better treated than they have been.

CORONER - It has been suggested that he was sometimes violent to them.

MRS. STAUNTON - Never, sir. He was like a tender father.

ARMITAGE - How about that riding switch? We've heard tales about that.

MRS. STAUNTON - Oh, it's you, Mr. Armitage? There are good reasons why you should make mischief against the Doctor. He told you what he thought of you and your canting ways.

CORONER - Now, then, I cannot have these recriminations. If I had known, Mr. Armitage, that there was personal feeling between the Doctor and you—

ARMITAGE - Nothing of the sort, sir. I'm doing my public duty.

CORONER - Well, the evidence of the witness seems very clear in combating your assertion of ill-treatment. Any other Juror? Very good, Mrs. Staunton.

(Exit MRS. STAUNTON into the servants' hall.)

Call Dr. Grimesby RYLOTT.

OFFICER - (calls at morning-room door) Dr. Rylott.

(Enter DR. RYLOTT.)

CORONER - Dr. Rylott, do you identify the body of the deceased as that of your stepdaughter, Violet Stonor?

RYLOTT - Yes, sir.

CORONER - Can you say anything which will throw any light upon this unhappy business?

RYLOTT - You may well say unhappy, sir. It has completely unnerved me.

CORONER - No doubt.

RYLOTT - She was the ray of sunshine in the house. She knew my ways. I am lost without her.

CORONER - No doubt. But we must confine ourselves to the facts. Have you any explanation which will cover the facts of your stepdaughter's death?

RYLOTT - I know just as much of the matter as you do. It is a complete and absolute mystery to me.

CORONER - Speaking as a doctor, you had no misgivings as to her health?

RYLOTT - She was never robust, but I had no reason for uneasiness.

CORONER - It has come out in evidence that her happiness had been affected by your interference with her engagement?

RYLOTT - (rising) That is entirely a misunderstanding sir. As a matter of fact I interfered in order to protect her from a man I had every reason to believe was a mere fortune hunter. She saw it herself in that light and was relieved to see the last of him.

CORONER - Excuse me sir but this introduces a new element into the case. Then the young lady had separate means?

RYLOTT - An annuity under her mother's will. (Sits.)

CORONER - And to whom does it now go?

RYLOTT - I believe that I might have a claim upon it but I am waiving it in favour of her sister.

CORONER - Very handsome I am sure.

(Murmurs from the JURY)

ARMITAGE - (rising) I expect sir so long as she lives under your roof you have the spending of it.

CORONER - Well, well, we can hardly go into that.

ARMITAGE - Had the young lady her own cheque book?

CORONER - Really Mr. Armitage you get away from the subject.

ARMITAGE - It is the subject.

RYLOTT - (rising) I am not here, sir, to submit to impertinence. (Sits.)

CORONER - I must ask you, Mr. Armitage—(Holds up hand.)

(ARMITAGE sits.)

Now, Dr. Rylott, the medical evidence, as you are aware, gives us no cause of death. You can suggest none?

RYLOTT - No, sir.

CORONER - Your stepdaughter has affirmed that her sister unlocked her door before appearing in the passage. Can you confirm this?

RYLOTT - Yes, I heard her unlock the door.

CORONER - You arrived in the passage simultaneously with the lady?

RYLOTT - Yes.

CORONER - You had been aroused by the scream?

RYLOTT - Yes.

CORONER - And naturally you came at once?

RYLOTT - Quite so. I was just in time to see her rush from her room and fall into her sister's arms. I can only imagine that she had some nightmare or hideous dream which had been too much for her heart. That is my own theory of her death.

CORONER - We have it on record that she said some incoherent words before she died.

RYLOTT - I heard nothing of the sort.

CORONER - She said nothing so far as you know?

RYLOTT - Nothing.

CORONER - Did you hear any music?

RYLOTT - Music, sir? No, I heard none.

CORONER - Well, what happened next?

RYLOTT - I satisfied myself that the poor girl was dead. Rodgers, my butler, had arrived, and together we laid her on her couch. I can really tell you nothing more.

CORONER - You did not at once send for a doctor?

RYLOTT - Well, sir, I was a doctor myself. To satisfy ENID I Consented in the morning to telegraph for Dr. Watson, who had been the girls' friend in India. I really could do no more.

CORONER - Looking back, you have nothing with which to reproach yourself in your treatment of this lady?

RYLOTT - She was the apple of my eye, I would have given my life for her.

CORONER - Well, gentlemen, any questions?

ARMITAGE - Yes, a good many. (Rising.)

(The other JURYMEN show some impatience.)

Well, I pay my way, the same as the rest of you, and I claim my rights. Mr. Coroner, I claim my rights.

CORONER - Well, well, Mr. Armitage, be as short as you can (Looks at his watch.) It is nearly two.

ARMITAGE - See here, Dr. Rylott, what about that great hound of yours? What about that whip you carry. What about the tales we hear down in the village of your bully-raggin' them young ladies?

RYLOTT - (rising) Really, Mr. Coroner, I must claim your protection. This fellow's impertinence is intolerable.

CORONER - You go rather far, Mr. Armitage. You must confine yourself to definite questions upon matters of fact.

(RYLOTT sits.)

ARMITAGE - Well, then, do you sleep with a light in your room?

RYLOTT - No, I do not.

ARMITAGE - How was you dressed in the passage?

RYLOTT - In my dressing-gown.

ARMITAGE - How did you get it?

RYLOTT - I struck a light, of course, and took it from a hook.

ARMITAGE - Well, if you did all that, how did you come into the passage as quick as the young lady who ran out just as she was?

RYLOTT - I can only tell you it was so.

ARMITAGE - Well, I can only tell you I don't believe it.

CORONER - You must withdraw that, Mr. Armitage.

ARMITAGE - I says what I mean, Mr. Coroner, and I say it again, I don't believe it. I've got common sense if I haven't got education.

RYLOTT - (rising) I can afford to disregard his remarks, Coroner.

CORONER - Anything else, Mr. Armitage?

ARMITAGE - I've said my say, and I stick to it.

CORONER - Then that will do, Dr. Rylott.

(Pause. DR. RYLOTT is going up towards the morning door.)

By the way, can your Indian servant help us at all in the matter?

RYLOTT - (coming down again) Ali sleeps in a garret and knew nothing till next morning. He is my personal valet.

CORONER - Then we need not call him. Very good, Dr. Rylott. you can remain if you wish. (To JURY.) Well, gentlemen, you have heard the evidence relating to this very painful case. There are several conceivable alternatives. There is death by murder. Of this I need not say there is not a shadow or tittle of evidence. There is death by suicide. Here, again, the presumption is absolutely against it. Then there is death by accident. We have nothing to lead us to believe that there has been an accident. Finally, we come to death by natural causes. It must be admitted that these natural causes are obscure, but the processes of nature are often mysterious, and we cannot claim to have such an exact knowledge of them that we can always define them. You have read the evidence of Professor Van Donop and you have heard that of Dr. Watson. If you are not satisfied it is always within your competence to declare that death arose from unknown causes. It is for you to form your own conclusions.

(The JURY buzz together for a moment. The CORONER looks at his watch, rises, and goes over to DR. RYLOTT.)

We are later than I intended.

RYLOTT - These absurd interruptions—!

CORONER - Yes, at these country inquests we generally have some queer fellows on the jury.

RYLOTT - Lunch must be ready. Won't you join us.

CORONER - Well, well, I shall be delighted.

FOREMAN - We are all ready, sir.

(CORONER returns to table.)

CORONER - Well, gentlemen? (Sits.)

FOREMAN - We are for unknown causes.

CORONER - Quite so. Unanimous?

ARMITAGE - No, sir. I am for further investigation. I don't say it's unknown and I won't say it's unknown.

CORONER - I entirely agree with the majority finding. Well, gentlemen that will finish our labours. Officer—

(The OFFICER comes to him. ARMITAGE sits.)

CORONER - You will all sign the inquisition before you leave this room officer will take your signatures as you pass out

(The JURY rise—sign book as they go out into the entrance hall.)

CORONER - (crossing to ARMITAGE) Mr. Armitage. One moment. Mr. Armitage, I am sorry that you are not yet satisfied.

ARMITAGE - No, sir, I am not.

CORONER - You are a little exacting (Turns away.)

RYLOTT - (touching ARMITAGE on the shoulder) I have only one thing to say to you sir. Get out of my house. Do you hear?

ARMITAGE - Yes Dr Rylott I hear. And I seem to hear something else. Something crying from the ground, Dr. Rylott, from the ground.

(Exits slowly into the entrance hall.)

RYLOTT - Impertinent rascal! (Turns away.)

(Enter WATSON, ENID and the other witnesses from the morning room. They all file out towards the entrance hall.)

(ENID has come down-stage. DR WATSON comes back from door.)

WATSON - Good bye Miss Enid (Shakes hands. Then in a lower voice) Don't forget that you have a friend.

(He goes out.)

(Business of CORONER and RYLOTT lighting cigarettes—ENID catches RYLOTT'S eye across CORONER and shrinks down onto a chair.)

CURTAIN

ACT II

Two years elapse between Acts I and II

SCENE I. DR. RYLOTT'S study at Stoke Place

The door at one side, a pair of French windows on the other. It is two years later.

Enter MRS. STAUNTON, showing in ARMITAGE.

MRS. STAUNTON - I can't tell how long the Doctor may be. It's not long since he went out.

ARMITAGE - Well, I'll wait for him, however long it is.

MRS. STAUNTON - It's nothing I could do for you, I suppose.

ARMITAGE - No, it is not.

MRS. STAUNTON - Well, you need not be so short. Perhaps, after you've seen the Doctor, you may be sorry.

ARMITAGE - There's the law of England watching over me, Mrs. Staunton. I advise you not to forget it—nor your master either. I fear no man so long as I am doing my duty.

(Enter ENID.)

Ah, Miss Stonor, I am very glad to see you.

ENID - (bewildered) Good-day, Mr. Armitage. What brings you up here?

ARMITAGE - I had a little business with the Doctor. But I should be very glad to have a chat with you also.

MRS. STAUNTON - I don't think the Doctor would like it, Miss Enid.

ARMITAGE - A pretty state of things. Isn't this young lady able to speak with whoever she likes? Do you call this a prison, or a private asylum, or what? These are fine doings in a free country.

MRS. STAUNTON - I am sure the Doctor would not like it.

ARMITAGE - Look here, Mrs. Staunton, two is company and three is none. If I'm not afraid of your master, I'm not afraid of YOU. You're a bit beyond your station, you are. Get to the other side of that door and leave us alone, or else—

MRS. STAUNTON - Or what, Mr. Armitage?

ARMITAGE - As sure as my father was a Methodist I'll go down to the J.P. and swear out an information that this young lady is under constraint.

MRS. STAUNTON - Oh—well, you need not be so hot about it. It's nothing to me what you say to Miss Enid. But the Doctor won't like it.

(She goes out.)

ARMITAGE - (looking at the door) You haven't such a thing as a hatpin? (Crossing over to door.)

ENID - No.

ARMITAGE - If I were to jab it through that keyhole—

ENID - Mr. Armitage please don't.

ARMITAGE - You'd hear Sister Jane's top note. But we'll speak low for I don't mean she shall hear. First of all Miss Enid are they using you? Are you all right?

ENID - Mr. Armitage I know you mean it all for kindness but I cannot discuss my personal affairs with you. I hardly know you.

ARMITAGE - Only the village grocer. I know all about that. But I've taken an interest in you Miss Stonor and I'm not the kind of man that can't leave go his hold. I came here not to see you, but your stepfather.

ENID - Oh, Mr. Armitage, I beg you to go away at once. You have no idea how violent he is if any one thwarts him. Please, please go at once.

ARMITAGE - Well Miss Stonor your only chance of getting to go is to answer my questions. When my conscience is clear, I'll go and not before. My conscience tells me that it is my duty to stay here till I have some satisfaction.

ENID - (crossing to settee and sitting) What is it, Mr. Armitage. Let's sit down.

ARMITAGE - (bringing chair over to settee) Well I'll tell you. I make it my business to know what is going on in this house. It may be that I like you or it may be that I dislike your stepfather. Or it may be that it is just my nature but so it is I've got my own ways of finding out, and I find out.

ENID - What have you found out?

ARMITAGE - Now look here, Miss. Cast your mind back to that inquest two years ago.

ENID - Oh! (Turning away.)

ARMITAGE - I'm sorry if it hurts you, but I must speak plain. When did your sister meet her death? It was shortly after her engagement was it not?

ENID - Yes, it was.

ARMITAGE - Well, you're engaged now, are you not?

ENID - Yes, I am.

ARMITAGE - Point number one. Well, now, have there not been repairs lately, and are you not forced to sleep in the very room your sister died in?

ENID - Only for a few nights.

ARMITAGE - Point number two. In your evidence you said you heard music in the house at night. Have you never heard music of late?

ENID - Good God! only last night I thought I heard it; and then persuaded myself that it was a dream. But how do you know these things, Mr. Armitage, and what do they mean?

ARMITAGE - Well, I won't tell you how I know them, and I can't tell you what they mean. But it's devilish, Miss Stonor, devilish! (Rising.) Now I've come up to see your stepfather and to tell him, as man to man, that I've got my eye on him, and that if anything happens to you it will be a bad day's work for him.

ENID - (rising) Oh, Mr. Armitage, he would beat you within an inch of your life. Mr. Armitage, you cannot think what he is like when the fury is on him. He is terrible.

ARMITAGE - The law will look after me.

ENID - It might avenge you, Mr. Armitage, but it could not protect you. Besides, there is no possible danger. You know of my engagement to Lieutenant Curtis?

ARMITAGE - I hear he leaves to-morrow.

ENID - That is true. But the next day I am going on a visit to his mother, at Fenton. Indeed, there is no danger.

ARMITAGE - Well, I won't deny that I am consoled by what you say, but there's just one condition on which I would leave this house.

ENID - What is that?

ARMITAGE - Well, I remember your friend, Dr. Watson, at the inquest – and we've heard of his connection with Mr. Sherlock HOLMES. If you'll promise me that you'll slip away to London to-morrow, see those two gentlemen, and get their advice, I'll wash my hands of it. I should feel that some one stronger than me Was looking after you.

ENID - Oh, Mr. Armitage, I couldn't.

ARMITAGE - (folding his arms) Then I stay here.

ENID - It is Lieutenant Curtis's last day in England.

ARMITAGE - When does he leave?

ENID - In the evening.

ARMITAGE - Well if you go in the morning you'd be back in time.

ENID - But how can I get away?

ARMITAGE - Who's to stop you? Have you money?

ENID - Yes, I have enough.

ARMITAGE - Then go.

ENID - It is really impossible.

ARMITAGE - (sitting) Very good. Then I'll have it out with Doctor.

ENID - (crossing to him) There, there! I'll promise. I'll go. I won't have you hurt I'll write and arrange it all somehow.

ARMITAGE - Word of honour?

ENID - Yes, yes I'll write to Dr Watson. Oh do go. This way. (Goes to the French window.) If you keep among the laurels you can get to the high road and no one will meet you.

ARMITAGE - (going up to the windows. Pause. Returning) That dog about?

ENID - It is with the Doctor. Oh do go! and thank you—Thank you with all my heart.

ARMITAGE - My wife and I can always take you in. Don't you forget it.

(ARMITAGE goes out ENID stands looking after him. As she does so MRS STAUNTON enters the room.)

MRS. STAUNTON - I saw Mr. Armitage going off through the shrubbery (Looks out of window.)

ENID - Yes he has gone.

MRS. STAUNTON - But why did he not wait to see the Doctor.

ENID - He's changed his mind.

MRS STAUNTON - He is the most impertinent busybody in the whole village. Fancy the insolence of him coming up here without a with-your- leave or by-your- leave. What was it he wanted, Miss Enid?

ENID - It is not your place, Mrs. Staunton, to ask such questions.

MRS. STAUNTON - Oh, indeed! For that matter, Miss Enid, I should not have thought it was your place to have secrets with the village grocer. The Doctor will want to know all about it.

ENID - What my stepfather may do is another matter. I beg, Mrs. Staunton, that you will attend to your own affairs and leave me alone.

MRS. STAUNTON - (putting her arms akimbo) High and mighty, indeed! I'm to do all the work of the house, but the grocer can come in and turn me out of the room. If you think I am nobody you may find yourself mistaken some of these days.

ENID - How dare you—(She makes for the door as RYLOTT enters.)

RYLOTT - Why, ENID, what's the matter? Any one been upsetting you? What's all this, Mrs. Staunton?

ENID - Mrs. Staunton has been rude to me.

RYLOTT - Dear, dear! Here's a storm in a teacup. Well, now, come and tell me all about it. No one shall bother my little Enid. What would her sailor boy say?

MRS. STAUNTON - Mr. Armitage has been here. He would speak with Miss ENID alone. I didn't think it right. That is why Miss Enid is offended.

RYLOTT - Where is the fellow?

MRS. STAUNTON - He is gone. He went off through the shrubbery.

RYLOTT - Upon my word, he seems to make himself at home. What did he want, ENID?

ENID - He wanted to know how I was.

RYLOTT - This is too funny! You have made a conquest, Enid. You have a rustic admirer.

ENID - I believe he is a true friend who means well to me.

RYLOTT - Astounding! Perhaps it is as well for him that he did not prolong his visit. But now, my dear girl, go to your room until I send for you. I am very sorry that you have been upset, and I will see that such a thing does not happen again. Tut, tut! my little girl shall not be worried. Leave it to me. (Goes up to door with ENID.)

(ENID goes out.)

Well, what is it, then? Why have you upset her?

MRS. STAUNTON - Why has she upset me? Why should I be always the last to be considered?

RYLOTT - Why should you be considered at all?

MRS. STAUNTON - You dare to say that to me—you that promised me marriage only a year ago. If I was what I should be, then there would be no talk as to who is the mistress of this house. I'll put up with no more of her tantrums, talking to me as if I were the kitchen-maid. (Turning from him.)

RYLOTT - You forget yourself.

MRS STAUNTON - I forget nothing. I don t forget your promise and it will be a bad day for you if you don't keep it.

RYLOTT - I'll put you out on the roadside if you dare speak so to me.

MRS STAUNTON - You will, will you? Try it and see. I saved you once. Maybe I could do the other thing if I tried.

RYLOTT - Saved me?

MRS. STAUNTON - Yes saved you. If it hadn't been for my evidence at that inquest that fellow Armitage would have taken the Jury with him. Yes he would. I've had it from them since.

RYLOTT - Well you only spoke the truth.

MRS. STAUNTON - The truth! Do you think I don't know?

RYLOTT - What do you know?

(She is silent and looks hard at him.)

What do you know?

(She is still silent.)

Don't look at me like that woman. What do you know?

MRS. STAUNTON - I know enough

(Pause.)

RYLOTT - Tell me then—how did she die?

MRS. STAUNTON - Only you know that. I may not know how she died but I know very well—

RYLOTT - (interrupting) You were always fanciful Kate but I know very well that you have only my own interests at heart. Put it out of your head if I have said anything unkind. Don't quarrel with this little fool, or you may interfere with my plans. Just wait a little longer and things will come straight with us. You know that I have a hasty temper but it is soon over.

MRS. STAUNTON - You can always talk me round, and you know it. Now, listen to me, for I am the only friend you've got. Don't try it again. You've got clear once. But a second would be too dangerous.

RYLOTT - They would make no more of the second than of the first. No one in the world can tell. It's impossible, I tell you. If she marries, half my income is gone.

MRS. STAUNTON - Yes, I know. Couldn't she sign it to you?

RYLOTT - She can be strong enough when she likes. She would never sign it to me. I hinted at it once, and she talked of a lawyer. (Pause.) But if anything should happen to her—well, there's an end to all our trouble.

MRS. STAUNTON - They must suspect.

RYLOTT - Let them suspect. But they can prove nothing.

MRS. STAUNTON - Not yet.

RYLOTT - On Wednesday she goes a-visiting, and who knows when she may return? No, it's to-morrow or never.

MRS. STAUNTON - Then let it be never.

RYLOTT - And lose half my income without a struggle? No, Kate, it's all or nothing with me now.

MRS. STAUNTON - Well, look out for Armitage.

RYLOTT - What about him?

MRS. STAUNTON - He must have known something before he dared to come here.

RYLOTT - What can he know of our affairs?

MRS. STAUNTON - There's Rodgers. You think he's half-witted. So he is. But he may know more and say more than we think. He talks and Armitage talks. Maybe Armitage gets hold of him.

RYLOTT - We'll soon settle that. (Crossing to bell-pull.) I'll twist the old rogue's neck if he has dared to play me false. There's one thing - - he can't hold anything in if I want it to come out. Did you ever see a snake and a white mouse? You just watch.

(Enter RODGERS.)

Come here, Rodgers.

RODGERS - Yes, sir.

RYLOTT - Stand here, where the light falls on your face, Rodgers. I shall know then if you are telling me the truth.

RODGERS - The truth, sir. Surely I would tell that.

RYLOTT - (takes chair from behind settee) Sit there! Don't move! Now look at me. That's right. You can't lie to me now. You've been down to see Mr. Armitage.

RODGERS - Sir—I hope—there was no harm in that.

RYLOTT - How often?

RODGERS - Two or three times.

RYLOTT - How often?

RODGERS - Two or three—

RYLOTT - How often?

RODGERS - When I go to the village I always see him.

MRS. STAUNTON - That's nearly every day.

RYLOTT - What have you told him about me?

RODGERS - Oh, sir, nothing.

RYLOTT - What have you told him?

RODGERS - Just the news of the house sir.

RYLOTT - What news?

RODGERS - Well, about Miss Enid's engagement, and Siva biting the gardener and the cook giving notice and the like.

RYLOTT - Nothing more than this?

RODGERS - No sir.

RYLOTT - Nothing more about Miss Enid?

RODGERS - No sir.

RYLOTT You swear it?

RODGERS - No, sir, no. I said nothing more.

RYLOTT - (springing up, catching him by the neck, shaking him) You doddering old rascal how came you to say anything at all? I kept you here out of charity and you dare to gossip about my affairs. I've had enough of you —(Throwing him off) I'll go to London tomorrow and get a younger man. You pack up your things and go. Do you hear?

RODGERS - Won't you look it over sir? I'm an old man sir. I have no place to go to. Where am I to go?

RYLOTT - You can go to the devil for all I care, or to your friend Armitage the grocer. There is no place for you here. Get out of the room.

RODGERS - Yes sir. You won't reconsider it?

RYLOTT - Get out. And tell Miss Enid I want her.

RODGERS - Yes, sir.

(RODGERS goes out.)

MRS. STAUNTON - You have done wisely. He was not safe.

RYLOTT - The old devil suited me too in a way. A younger man may give more trouble.

MRS. STAUNTON - You'll soon break him in.

RYLOTT - Yes, I expect I will. (Crossing to her.) Now, make it right with ENID for my sake. You must play the game to the end.

MRS. STAUNTON - It's all right. I'm ready for her.

(Enter ENID.)

RYLOTT - My dear, Mrs. Staunton is very sorry if she has given you any annoyance. I hope you will accept her apology in the same spirit that it is offered.

MRS. STAUNTON - I meant no harm, Miss Enid, and I was only thinking of the master's interests. I hope you'll forgive me.

ENID - Certainly, I forgive you, Mrs. Staunton.

RYLOTT - There's a good little girl. Now, Mrs. Staunton, you had better leave us.

(MRS. STAUNTON goes out.)

Now, my dear, you must not be vexed with poor Mrs. Staunton, for she is a very hard-working woman and devoted to her duty, though, of course, her manners are often wanting in polish. Come now, dear, say that it is All right.

(ENID sits on settee.)

ENID - I have said that I forgive her.

RYLOTT - You must tell me anything I can do, to make you happier. Of course, you have some one else now, but I would not like you to forget your old stepfather altogether. Until the day when you have to leave me, I wish to do the very best for you.

ENID - You are very kind.

RYLOTT - Can you suggest anything that I can do?

ENID - No, no, there is nothing.

RYLOTT - I was a little too rough last week. I am sorry for that. I should wish your future husband to like me. You will tell him, when you see him, that I have done what I could to make you happy?

ENID - Yes, yes.

RYLOTT - You see him to-morrow?

ENID - Yes.

RYLOTT - And he leaves us to-morrow evening? (Sitting beside her on settee.)

ENID - Yes.

RYLOTT - You have all my sympathy, dear. But he will soon back again, and then, of course, you will part no more. You will be sorry to hear that old Rodgers has been behaving badly, and that I must get rid of him.

ENID - (rising) Rodgers! What has he done?

RYLOTT - He grows more foolish and incompetent every day. I propose to go to London myself tomorrow to get a new butler. Would you send a line in my name to the agents to say that I shall call about two o clock?

ENID - I will do so.

RYLOTT - There's a good little girl (Pause. Crossing to her and placing his hand on her shoulder) There's nothing on your mind, is there?

ENID - Oh no.

RYLOTT - Well then run away and get your letter written. I dare bet you have another of your own to write. One a day—or two a day? – what is his Allowance? Well, well, we have All done it at some time.

(Enter ALI with milk jug glass and saucer on a tray.)

ALI - I beg pardon Sahib, I go.

RYLOTT - Come in! Come in! Put my milk down on the table.

(ALI does so.)

Now my dear please don't forget to write the letter to the agents.

(ENID goes out.)

You fool! Why did you not make sure I was alone?

ALI - I thought no one here but Sahib.

RYLOTT - Well as it happens there's no harm done (Goes to door and locks it. Pulls down blind of window.)

(While he does so ALI opens a cupboard and takes out a square wicker work basket.RYLOTT pours milk into saucer and puts it before basket. Then he cracks his fingers and whistles while ALI plays on an Eastern flute.)

CURTAIN

SCENE II. Mr. Sherlock Holmes' Room in Baker Street

(Enter BILLY, showing in DR. WATSON.)

WATSON - I particularly want to see Mr. Holmes.

BILLY - Well, sir, I expect he will be back almost immediately.

WATSON - Is he very busy just now?

BILLY - Yes, sir, we are very busy. We don't get much time to ourselves these days.

WATSON - Any particular case?

BILLY - Quite a number of cases, sir. Two German princes and the Duchess of Ferrers yesterday. The Pope's been bothering us again. Wants us to go to Rome over the cameo robbery. We are very overworked.

WATSON - Well, I'll wait for Mr. Holmes.

BILLY - Very good, sir. Here is The Times. There's four for him in the waiting- room now.

WATSON - Any lady among them?

BILLY - Not what I would call a lady, sir.

WATSON - All right, I'll wait. (Lights a cigarette and looks around him.) Just the same as ever. There are the old chemicals! Heavens! what have I not endured from those chemicals in the old days? Pistol practice on the wall. Quite so. I wonder if he still keeps tobacco in that Persian slipper? Yes, here it is. And his pipes in the coal- scuttle—black clays. Full of them—the same as ever. (Takes one out and smells it.) Faugh! Bottle of cocaine—Billy, Billy!

BILLY - I've done my best to break him of it, sir.

WATSON - All right, Billy, you can go.

(BILLY goes out.)

There's the old violin—the same old violin, with one string left. (Sits on settee.)

(Enter SHERLOCK HOLMES, disguised as a workman, with tools.)

HOLMES - You sent for me, Mr. Sherlock Holmes.

WATSON - I am not Mr. Holmes.

HOLMES - Beg pardon, sir, it was to mend the gas-bracket.

WATSON - What's wrong with it?

HOLMES - Leaking sir.

WATSON - Well go on with your work.

HOLMES - Yes, sir. (Goes to the bracket.) Hope I won't disturb you sir?

WATSON - (taking up "The Times") That's all right Don't mind me.

HOLMES - Very untidy man Mr. Holmes sir.

WATSON - What do you mean by that?

HOLMES - Well, sir, you can't help noticing it. It's all over the room. I've 'eard say he was as tidy as any when he started, but he learned bad 'abits from a cove what lived with him. Watson was his name.

(Slips into bedroom.)

WATSON - (rising) You impertinent fellow! How dare you talk in such a fashion? What do you want? (Looks round.) Why! wha' deuce has become of him?

(The workman emerges as SHERLOCK HOLMES, in dressing-gown with hands in pockets.)

Good Heavens Holmes! I should never have recognized you.

HOLMES - My dear Watson when you begin to recognize me it will indeed be the beginning of the end. When your eagle eye penetrates my disguise I shall retire to an eligible poultry farm.

WATSON - But why—?

HOLMES - A case my dear Watson a case! One of those small conundrums which a trustful public occasionally confides to my investigation. To the British workman, Watson, all doors are open. His costume is unostentatious and his habits are sociable. A tool bag is an excellent passport and a tawny moustache will secure the co-operation of the maids. It may interest you to know that my humble double is courting a cook at Battersea. (Strikes match and lights pipe.)

WATSON - My dear Holmes! Is it fair to the girl?

HOLMES - Chivalrous old Watson! It's a game of life and death, and every card must be played! But in this case I have a hated rival—the constable on the adjoining beat—so when I disappear, all will readjust itself. We walk out on Saturday evenings. Oh! those walks! But the honour of a Duchess is at stake. A mad world, my masters. (Turns to survey WATSON.) Well, Watson, what is your news?

WATSON - (smiling) Well, Holmes, I came here to tell you what I am sure will please you.

HOLMES - Engaged, Watson, engaged! Your coat, your hat, your gloves, your buttonhole, your smile, your blush! The successful suitor shines from you all over. What I had heard of you or perhaps what I had not heard of you, had already excited my worst suspicions. (Looks fixedly at WATSON.) But this is better and better, for I begin to perceive that it is a young lady whom I know and respect.

WATSON - But, Holmes, this is marvellous. The lady is Miss Morstan, whom you have indeed met and admired. But how could you tell—

HOLMES - By the same observation, my dear Watson, which assures me that you have seen the lady this morning. (Picks a hair off WATSON'S breast, wraps it round his finger, and glances at it with his lens.) Charming, my dear fellow, charming. There is no mistaking the Titian tint. You lucky fellow! I envy you.

WATSON - Thank you, Holmes. Some of these days I may find myself congratulating you.

HOLMES - No marriage without love, Watson.

WATSON - Then why not love? (Placing his hand on HOLMES'S shoulders.)

HOLMES - Absurd, Watson, absurd! I am not for love, nor love for me. It would disturb my reason, unbalance my faculties. Love is like a flaw in the crystal, sand in the clockwork, iron near the magnet. No, no, I have other work in the world.

WATSON - You have, indeed. Billy says you are very busy just now.

HOLMES - There are one or two small matters.

WATSON - Have you room to consider one other—the case of Miss Enid Stonor?

HOLMES - My dear fellow, if you have any personal interest in it. (Sitting on divan.)

WATSON - Yes, I feel keenly about it.

HOLMES - (taking out note-book) Let us see how I stand. There is the Baxter Square murder—I have put the police on the track. The Clerkenwell Jewel Robbery—that is now clearing. The case of the Duchess of Ferrers—I have my material. The Pope's cameos. His Holiness must wait. The Princess who is about to run from home—let her run. I must see one or two who are waiting for me—(rings bell)—then I am entirely at your disposal.

(Enter BILLY.)

BILLY - Yes, Mr. Holmes.

HOLMES - How many are waiting?

BILLY - Three, sir.

HOLMES - A light morning. Show them in now.

(BILLY goes out.)

WATSON - Well, I'll look in later.

HOLMES - (striking match and lighting pipe) No, no, my dear fellow! I have always looked on you as a partner in the Firm—Holmes, Watson, Billy & Co. That's our brass plate when we raise one. If you'll sit there I shall soon be free.

(Enter BILLY, with a card on tray. MR HOLT LOAMING follows, a rich, dissipated-looking, middle-aged man in an astrakhan-collared coat. BILLY goes out.)

HOLMES - (reading) Mr. Holt Loaming. I remember the name. A racing man, I believe?

LOAMING - Yes, sir.

HOLMES - Pray take a seat.

(LOAMING draws up near the table.)

What can I do for you?

LOAMING - Time's money, Mr. Holmes, both yours and mine. I'm pretty quick off the mark, and you won't mind that. I'm not here on the advice gratis line. Don't you think it. I've my cheque book here—(takes it out)—and there's plenty behind it. I won't grudge you your fee, Mr. Holmes. I promise you that.

HOLMES - Well, Mr. Loaming, let us hear the business.

LOAMING - My wife, Mr. Holmes—damn her!—she's given me the slip. Got back to her own people and they've hid her. There's the law, of course, but she'd get out all kinds of lies about ill-treatment. She's mine, and I'll just take her when I know where to lay my hands on her.

HOLMES - How would you take her?

LOAMING - I just have to walk up to her and beckon. She's one of those wincing kind of nervous fillies that kick about in the paddock but give in when once the bridle's on them and they feel the whip. You show me where she is, and I'll do the rest.

HOLMES - She is with her own people, you say?

LOAMING - Well, there's no man in the case, if that's what you're driving at. Lord! if you knew how straight she is, and how she carries on when I have a fling. She's got a cluster of aunts, and she's lyin' low somewhere among them. It's for you to put her up.

HOLMES - I fancy not, Mr. Loaming.

LOAMING - Eh? What's that?

HOLMES - I rather like to think of her among that cluster of aunts.

LOAMING - But, damn it, sir, she's my wife.

HOLMES - That's why!

LOAMING - (getting up) Well, it's a rum start, this. Look here, you don't know what you're missing. I'd have gone to five hundred. Here's the cheque.

HOLMES - The case does not attract me. (Rings bell.)

(Enter BILLY.)

Show Mr. Loaming out, Billy.

LOAMING - It's the last you'll see of me, Mr. Holmes.

HOLMES - Life is full of little consolations.

LOAMING - Damn!

(He takes his hat and goes out with BILLY.)

HOLMES - I'm afraid I shall never be a rich man, Watson.

(Re-enter BILLY.)

Well?

BILLY - Mr. James B. Montague, sir.

(Enter MONTAGUE, as BILLY goes out.)

HOLMES - Good morning, Mr. Montague. Pray take a chair.

(MONTAGUE sits.)

What can I do?

MONTAGUE - (a furtive-looking man with slimy ways) Anything fresh about the sudden death of my brother, sir? The police said it was murder, and you said it was murder; but we don't get any further, do we? (Placing hat on floor.)

HOLMES - I have not lost sight of it.

MONTAGUE - That man Henderson was a bad man, Holmes, an evil liver and a corruption. Yes, sir, a corruption a danger. Who knows what passed between them? I've suspicions—I've always had my suspicions.

HOLMES - So you said.

MONTAGUE - Have you worked any further on that line, sir? Because, if you tell me from time to time how it is shaping, I may be able to give you a word in season.

HOLMES - I have my eye on him—a very cunning rascal, as you say. We have not enough to arrest him on, but we work away in the hope.

MONTAGUE - Good, Mr. Holmes, good! Watch him; you'll get him, as safe as Judgment.

HOLMES - I'll let you know if anything comes of it. (Rings.)

MONTAGUE - (rising) That's right, sir. Watch 'im. I'm his brother, sir. It's me that should know. It's never out of my mind.

(Enter BILLY.)

HOLMES - Very good, Mr. Montague. Good-morning.

(MONTAGUE and BILLY go out.)

Curious little murder, Watson; done for most inadequate motive. That was the murderer.

WATSON - Good Heavens!

HOLMES - My case is almost complete. Meanwhile I amuse him and myself by the pretended pursuit of the wrong man—an ancient device, Watson.

(Re-enter BILLY.)

Well, any more?

BILLY - Mr. Milverton is here, Mr. Holmes.

HOLMES - Show him in when I ring.

(BILLY goes out.)

I am sorry to delay the business upon which you wished to consult me; but this, I hope, will be the last. You remember Milverton?

WATSON - No.

HOLMES - Ah! it was after your time. The most crawling reptile in London —the King of the Blackmailers—a cunning, ruthless devil. I have traced seventeen suicides to that man's influence. It is he who is after the Duchess of Ferrers.

WATSON - The beautiful Duchess, whose re-marriage is announced?

HOLMES - Exactly. He has a letter which he thinks would break off the wedding. (Rings.) It is my task to regain it.

(Enter MILVERTON.)

HOLMES - Well, Mr. Milverton. Pray take a seat.

MILVERTON - Who is this?

HOLMES - My friend, Dr. Watson. Do you mind?

MILVERTON - (sitting) Oh! I have no object in secrecy. It is your client's reputation, not mine, which is at stake.

HOLMES - Your reputation! Good Heavens! (Crossing to fireplace and filling pipe from slipper.)

MILVERTON - Not much to lose there, is there, Mr. Holmes? I can't be hurt. But she can. Hardly a fair fight, is it?

HOLMES - What are the terms now? (Filling pipe.)

MILVERTON - Steady at seven thousand. No money—no marriage.

HOLMES - Suppose she tells the whole story to the Marquis? Then your letter is not worth sixpence. He would condone all. Come, now, what harm is in the letter?

MILVERTON - Sprightly—very sprightly. However, it is purely a matter of business. If you think it is in the best interests of your client that the Marquis should see the letter—why, you would be very foolish to pay a large sum to regain it.

HOLMES - The lady has no great resources.

MILVERTON - But her marriage is a most suitable time for her friends and relations to make some little effort. I can assure you that this envelope would give more joy than all the tiaras and bracelets in Regent Street.

HOLMES - No, it is impossible!

MILVERTON - Dear me! Dear me! How unfortunate.

HOLMES - It can profit you in no way to push matters to an end.

MILVERTON - There you mistake. I have other cases maturing. If it were known that I had been severe on the Duchess the others would be more open to reason.

HOLMES - Well, well, you give us till noon to-morrow? (Rings.)

MILVERTON - But not an hour longer.

(Enter BILLY.)

HOLMES - We are at your mercy. Surely you won't treat us too harshly?

MILVERTON - Not a minute longer. (Putting on hat.)

(BILLY and MILVERTON go out.)

Terrible! Terrible! A fumigator would be useful, eh, Watson – Pah!

WATSON - What can you do?

HOLMES - My dear Watson—what have I done? It is this gentleman's cook who has honoured me. In the intervals of philandering, I have made an acquaintance with the lock on the safe. Mr. Milverton spent last night at his club; when he returns home he will find there has been a little burglary at The Battersea, and his precious letter is missing. (Rings.)

WATSON - Holmes, you are splendid!

(Enter BILLY.)

HOLMES - Tut, tut! (To BILLY.) Well, any more?

BILLY - One lady, sir—just come—Miss Enid Stonor, of Stoke Moran.

WATSON - Ah! this is the case. (Rising.)

HOLMES - I'll ring, Billy.

(BILLY goes out.)

Now, Watson! Stonor! Stonor! Surely I associate the name with something?

WATSON - I told you of the case at the time. Sudden mysterious death of a girl at an old house in Stoke Moran, some two years ago.

HOLMES - My dear fellow! it all comes back to me. An inquest was it not, with a string of most stupid and ineffectual witnesses.

WATSON - I was one of them.

HOLMES - Of course—so you were, so you were. I docketed the evidence. It introduced to my notice a gentleman of singular and most interesting personality. I have a few notes. (Takes down a scrapbook from a row.) Let's see—it's R—Ranter—Roma – Rylott! That's our man. Fifty-five years of age, killed his khitmutgar in India; once in a madhouse, married money—wife died - - distinguished surgeon. Well, Watson, what has the distinguished surgeon been up to now? (Throwing scrapbook on divan.)

WATSON - Devilry, I fear.

HOLMES - I have the case very clear in my mind.

WATSON - Then you may remember that the death of the lady followed close upon her engagement?

HOLMES - Exactly.

WATSON - Miss Enid Stonor in turn became engaged, about a month ago, to a neighbour, Lieutenant Curtis.

HOLMES - Ah!

WATSON - Unhappily, the young man leaves for the Mediterranean to- day. She will henceforward be alone at Stoke Moran.

HOLMES - I see.

WATSON - And some circumstances have excited her alarm.

HOLMES - I gather that the amiable stepfather stands to lose in case of a marriage.

WATSON - That is so. Of course, supposing that Rylott did the other girl to death, it seems unlikely, on the face of it, that he would try it on again, as two sudden deaths in the house could hardly pass the coroner—

HOLMES - No, no, Watson! you are making the mistake of putting your normal brain into Rylott's abnormal being. The born criminal is often a monstrous egotist. His mind is unhinged from the beginning. What he wants he must have. Because he thinks a thing, it is right. Because he does a thing, it will escape detection. You can't say a priori that he will take this view or that one. Perhaps we had best have the young lady in. (Rings bell.) My dear fellow, you'll get into trouble if you go about righting the wrongs of distressed damsels. It won't do, Watson, it really won't.

(Enter ENID. WATSON gets up and meets her.)

WATSON - How do you do, Miss Enid? This is my friend, Mr. Holmes, of whom I spoke.

(HOLMES shakes hands with ENID.)

HOLMES - How do you do, Miss Stonor? Dear me! you must find a dog- cart a cold conveyance in this weather.

ENID - A dog-cart, Mr. Holmes?

HOLMES - One can hardly fail to observe the tell-tale splashes on the left sleeve. A white horse and clay soil are indicated. But what is this? You are trembling. Do sit down.

ENID - (looking round and sitting on settee) Tell me, Mr. Holmes, my stepfather has not been here?

HOLMES - No.

ENID - He saw me in the street. I dashed past him in a cab. he saw me; our eyes met, and he waved me to stop.

HOLMES - Why is your stepfather in London?

ENID - He came up on business.

HOLMES - It would be interesting to know what the business was.

ENID - It was to get a new butler. Rodgers, our old one, leave us, and a new butler is to come at once. I doubt if any servant would come to such a place.

HOLMES - He may certainly find some difficulty. He would, no doubt, apply to an agent.

ENID - At two o'clock, to Patterson and Green, of Cavendish Street.

HOLMES - Exactly. I know them. But this is a digression, is it not? We get back to the fact that he saw you in the street?

ENID - Yes, it was in Pall Mall. I fancy he followed me.

HOLMES - Would he imagine you would come here?

ENID - No, he would think I was going to Dr. Watson's. He knows that Dr. Watson is my only friend in London.

HOLMES - What has been Dr. Ryolott's attitude towards you your engagement?

ENID - He has been much kinder, because he knows I have one to protect me. But even so, there are moments— (Raises her arm.)

HOLMES - Good Heavens!

ENID - He does not realize his own strength. When he is angry he is like a fierce wild beast. Only last week he thrashed the blacksmith.

HOLMES - He is welcome to the blacksmith, but not to my clients. This must not occur again. Does your fiancé know of this?

ENID - I would not dare to tell him. He would do something dreadful. Besides, as I say, my stepfather has, on the whole, been kinder. But there is a look in his eyes, when I turn on him suddenly, that chills me to the bone. His kindness is from his head, not from his heart. I feel as if he were waiting—waiting—

HOLMES - Waiting for what?

ENID - Waiting for my fiancé to leave. Waiting till he has me at his mercy. That room freezes my blood. Often I cannot sleep for horror.

WATSON - What? He has changed your room? (Rising from armchair.)

ENID - My old room is under repair.

WATSON - You sleep, then, in the room where your sister died?

ENID - In the same room. And other things have happened. The music has come again.

HOLMES - The music? Tell me about this music.

ENID - It came before my sister's death. She spoke of it, and then I heard it myself the night she died. But it has come again. Oh, Mr. Holmes, I am terrified.

HOLMES - There, there! you've had enough to break any one's nerve. This —music—does it seem to be inside the house or outside?

ENID - Indeed, I could not say.

HOLMES - What is it like?

ENID - A sort of soft, droning sound.

HOLMES - Like a flute or pipe?

ENID - Yes. It reminds me of my childhood in India.

HOLMES - Ah—India?

ENID - And there's one other thing that puzzles me—my sister's dying words—as she lay in my arms she gasped out two words.

HOLMES - What were they?

ENID - "Band" and "Speckled."

HOLMES - Band—speckled—and Indian music. You sleep with your door and window fastened?

ENID - Yes, but so did poor Violet. It did not save her, and it may not save me.

HOLMES - Could there be anything in the nature of secret doors or panels?

ENID - No. I have searched again and again. There is nothing.

HOLMES - And nothing peculiar in the room?

ENID - No, I cannot say there is.

HOLMES - I must really drop in and have a look at this most interesting apartment. Suggestive—very suggestive. (Pause) When did you hear this music last?

ENID - Last night.

HOLMES - And your fiancé leaves to-day?

ENID - He leaves to-day. What shall I do?

HOLMES - Well, Miss Stonor, I take up your case. It presents features which commend it to me. You must put yourself into my hands.

ENID - I do—unreservedly. (Rising, and crossing to him.)

HOLMES - (to Watson) It is a question whether we are justified in letting her return at all to Stoke Moran.

ENID - I must return. At five o'clock my fiancé leaves, and I shall not see him again for months.

HOLMES - Ah! that is a complication. Where is the A.B.C.? (Finds it in umbrella stand.) Stonehouse—Stowell—Stoke—

ENID - I know my train, Mr. Holmes.

HOLMES - I was looking for mine.

ENID - You are coming down?

HOLMES - I shall not be content until I have seen this room of yours. Yes, that will do. I could get up to you between eleven and twelve, to- night. Would you have the goodness to leave your shutter open? The room is, I understand, upon the ground floor?

ENID - Oh! Mr. Holmes, it is not safe. You cannot think of the danger.

HOLMES - I have taken up your case, Miss Stonor, and this is part of it. Have you any friends in Stoke Moran?

ENID - Mr. Armitage and his wife.

HOLMES - That is most fortunate. Now, listen to me, Miss Stonor. When you have returned home certain circumstances may arise which will ensure your safety. In that case you will at Stoke Place until I come in the evening. On the other hand, things may miscarry, and you may not be safe. In that case I will so manage that a warning will reach you. You will then break from home and take refuge with the Armitages. Is that clear?

ENID - Who will bring me the warning?

HOLMES - I cannot say. But you have my assurance that it will come.

ENID - Then, until it does, I will stay at Stoke Place.

HOLMES - And should any new development occur you could always send me a telegram, could you not?

ENID - Yes, I could do that.

HOLMES - Then it is not goodbye, but au revoir.

(Enter BILLY.)

What is it?

BILLY - Please, Mr. Holmes, a gentleman to see you, at once.

HOLMES - Who is he?

BILLY - A very impatient gentleman, sir. It was all I could do to get him to stay in the waiting-room.

ENID - Is he tall, dark, with a black beard, and a long white scar on his cheek?

BILLY - That's him, Miss.

ENID - Oh, Mr. Holmes, what shall I do? He has followed me.

WATSON - If he went to my rooms, my landlady had instructions to send any one on here.

HOLMES - Exactly.

ENID - Oh! I dare not meet him, I dare not. Can't I slip out somehow?

HOLMES - I see no reason why you should stay. Billy, show the lady out by the side passage.

BILLY - Don't be alarmed, Miss, I'll see you through.

(BILLY and ENID go out.)

WATSON - This fellow is dangerous, Holmes. You may need a weapon.

HOLMES - There's something of the kind in that drawer at your right.

(Enter BILLY.)

BILLY - Shall I stay when I show him in, Mr. Holmes?

HOLMES - Why so?

BILLY - An ugly customer, Mr. Holmes.

HOLMES - Tut, tut! show him up.

(BILLY goes out.)

Well, Watson I must thank you for a most interesting morning. You are certainly the stormy petrel of crime.

(Enter DR RYLOTT)

RYLOTT - This is Mr. Sherlock Holmes I believe.

HOLMES - Your belief is justified.

RYLOTT - I have reason to think that you have taken unsolicited interest in my affairs.

HOLMES - Your name being—?

RYLOTT - My name, sir, is Grimesby Rylott—Doctor Grimesby Rylott, of Stoke Moran. (Throws down card.)

HOLMES - A pretty place, I hear! And obviously good for the lungs.

RYLOTT - Sir, you are trifling with me. I have come here to ask whether you have had a visit from my stepdaughter, Miss Enid Stonor—

HOLMES - The first law in my profession, Doctor, is never to answer questions.

RYLOTT - Sir, you shall answer me.

HOLMES - We could do with warmer weather.

RYLOTT - I insist upon an answer.

HOLMES - But I hear the crocuses are coming on.

RYLOTT - Curse your crocuses! I've heard of you, you meddling busybody. And you, Dr. Watson—I expected to find you here. What do you mean by interfering with my lawful affairs?

WATSON - So long as they are lawful, Dr. Rylott, no one is likely to interfere with them.

RYLOTT - Now look here, Mr. Holmes, perhaps I may seem to you a little hot- headed—

HOLMES - Dear me, Dr. Rylott, what put that idea into your head?

RYLOTT - I apologize if I have seemed rude—(Sitting)

HOLMES - Robust—a little robust—nothing more.

RYLOTT - I wish to put the matter to you as man to man. You know what girls are, how sudden and unreasonable their prejudices may be. Imagine, sir, how hurt I should feel to be distrusted by one whom I have loved.

HOLMES - You have my deep sympathy, Dr. Rylott.

RYLOTT - (pleased) Ah!

HOLMES - You are a most unfortunate man. There was that tragedy two years ago—

RYLOTT - Yes, indeed!

HOLMES - I think I could help you in that matter.

RYLOTT - How so?

HOLMES - As a friend, and without a fee.

RYLOTT - You are very good.

HOLMES - I am very busy, but your case seems so hard that I will put everything aside to assist you.

RYLOTT - In what way, sir?

HOLMES - I will come down at once, examine the room in which the tragedy occurred, and see if such small faculties as I possess can throw any light upon the matter.

RYLOTT - Sir, this is an intolerable liberty. (Rising.)

HOLMES - What! you don't want help?

RYLOTT - It is intolerable, I say. What I ask you to do—what I order you to do is to leave my affairs alone. Alone, sir—do you hear me?

HOLMES - You are perfectly audible.

RYLOTT - I'll have no interference—none! Don't dare to meddle with me. D'you hear, the pair of you? You—Holmes, I'm warning you.

HOLMES - (looking at his watch) I fear I must end this interview. Time flies when one is chatting. Life has its duties as well as its pleasures, Doctor.

RYLOTT - Insolent rascal! I'll—I'll—(Turns to the grate and picks up the poker.)

(WATSON jumps up.)

HOLMES - No, Watson, no! It does need poking, but perhaps you would put on a few coals first.

RYLOTT - You laugh at me? You don't know the man you are dealing with. You think that my strength fails because my hair is turned. I was the strongest man in India once. See that! (Bends the poker and throws it down at HOLMES' feet.) I am not a safe man to play with, Mr. Holmes.

HOLMES - Nor am I a safe man to play with, Dr. Rylott. Let me see – what were we talking about before the Sandow performance?

RYLOTT - You shall not overcrow me with your insolence! I tell you now, and you, too, Dr. Watson, that you interfere with my affairs to your own danger. You have your warning.

HOLMES - I'll make a note of it.

RYLOTT - And you refuse to tell me if Miss Stonor has been here?

HOLMES - Don't we seem to be travelling just a little in a circle?

RYLOTT - (picking up hat from table) Well, you can't prevent me from finding out from her.

HOLMES - Ah! there I must talk a little seriously to you Grimesby Rylott. You have mentioned this young lady, and I know something of her circumstances. I hold you responsible. My eye is on you sir and the Lord help you—the Lord help you if any harm befall her. Now leave this room, and take my warning with you.

RYLOTT - You cursed fool! I may teach you both not to meddle with what does not concern you. Keep clear of Stoke Moran!

(RYLOTT goes out slamming the door)

HOLMES - I had a presentiment he would slam the door.

(WATSON rises.)

Stoke Moran must be less dull than many country villages. Quite a breezy old gentleman Watson. Well I must thank you for a pretty problem. What the exact danger may be which destroyed one sister and now threatens the other may be suspected, but cannot yet be defined. That is why I must visit the room.

WATSON - I will come with you Holmes.

HOLMES - My dear fellow you are no longer an unattached knight- errant. Dangerous quests are forbidden. What would Morstan say?

WATSON - She would say that the man who would desert his friend would never make a good husband.

HOLMES - Well, my dear Watson, it may be our last adventure together, so I welcome your co-operation.

WATSON - Well, I'll be off.

HOLMES - You will leave Victoria to night at eleven fifteen, for Stoke Moran.

WATSON - Good bye—I'll see you at the station.

HOLMES - Perhaps you will.

(WATSON goes.)

Perhaps you will! (Rings.) Perhaps you won't! (Stands near fire.)

(Enter BILLY.)

BILLY - Yes, sir.

HOLMES - Ever been in love Billy?

BILLY - Not of late years, sir.

HOLMES - Too busy, eh?

BILLY - Yes, Mr. Holmes.

HOLMES - Same here. Got my bag there, Billy?

BILLY - Yes, sir. (Puts it on table.)

HOLMES - Put in that revolver.

BILLY - Yes, sir.

HOLMES - And the pipe and pouch.

BILLY - (takes it from table) Yes, sir.

HOLMES - Got the dark lantern?

BILLY - Yes, sir.

HOLMES - The lens and the tape?

BILLY - Yes, sir.

HOLMES - Plaster of Paris, for prints?

BILLY - Yes, sir.

HOLMES - Oh, and the cocaine. (Hands it.)

BILLY - Yes, sir. (Throws it down.)

HOLMES - You young villain! you've broken it. (Takes his ear and turns his head round.) You're a clever boy, Billy.

BILLY - Yes, Mr. Holmes.

CURTAIN.

ACT III

SCENE 1. The Hall of Stoke Place

MRS STAUNTON is discovered at the back reading a telegram.

MRS. STAUNTON - Are you there, Rodgers?

(Enter RODGERS)

RODGERS - Well, Mrs. Staunton.

MRS. STAUNTON - I've had a telegram from the master. He will be here presently. He is bringing the new butler with him so you can hand over to night.

RODGERS - To night, Mrs Staunton. It all seems very sudden.

MRS. STAUNTON - Peters will need your room. That's his name, Peters. He brings a young girl with him, his daughter. The attic will do for her. That will do Rodgers.

(RODGERS goes into the morning room.)

(Enter ENID from the entrance hall.)

ENID - Oh, Mrs Staunton.

MRS. STAUNTON - Yes, Miss.

ENID - Has any message come in my absence?

MRS. STAUNTON - No, Miss.

ENID - Let me know at once if any comes.

(ENID goes into the bedroom wing.)

MRS. STAUNTON - Yes Miss. A message! A message!

(Enter ALI hurriedly.)

MRS STAUNTON - (to him) Well?

ALI - Has she come back?

MRS. STAUNTON - Yes, she is in her room.

ALI - I see her meet Curtis Sahib. Then I lose her.

MRS. STAUNTON - Well, she has come back. I have heard from the master. She is not to go out any more. He will come soon. Until he does, we must hold her. She asked if there was a message for her. Who can she expect a message from? Ah—stand back, Ali, she's coming.

(ALI stands at door to servants' hall.)

(Re-enter ENID, still dressed for walking.)

MRS. STAUNTON - I beg pardon, Miss, but what are you going to do?

ENID - I am going down to the village. (Crosses towards entrance hall.)

MRS. STAUNTON - What for?

ENID - How dare you ask me such a question? What do you mean by it?

MRS. STAUNTON - I thought it was something we could do for you.

ENID - It was not.

MRS. STAUNTON - Then I am sorry, Miss, but it can't be done. The Doctor didn't like you going to London to-day. His orders are that you should not go out again.

ENID - How dare you? I am going out now.

MRS. STAUNTON - Get to the door, Ali! It's no use, Miss, we must obey our orders. You don't budge from here.

ENID - What is the meaning of this?

MRS. STAUNTON - It is not for the likes of us to ask the meaning. The Doctor is a good master, but his servants have to obey him.

ENID - I will go out. (Tries to rush past.)

MRS. STAUNTON - Lock the door, Ali.

(ALI locks the door to the entrance hall.)

The other locks are locked as well. You needn't try the windows, for Siva is loose. All right, Ali, give me the key—you can go!

(ALI goes into the servants' hall.)

Now, Miss, do what the Doctor wishes. That's my advice to you.

(She exits into the servants' hall.)

(ENID waits until she has gone; then she rushes across to the writing- and scribbles a telegram.)

(RODGERS enters from the morning-room.)

ENID - Oh, Rodgers—

RODGERS - Yes, Miss.

ENID - Come here, Rodgers!

(RODGERS comes down.)

I want to speak to you. I hear that you are leaving us. I wanted say how sorry I am.

RODGERS - God bless you, Miss Enid. My heart is sore to part with you. All the kindness I've ever had in this house has from poor Miss Violet and you.

ENID - Rodgers, if ever I have done anything for you, you can repay it now a hundredfold.

RODGERS - Nothing against the master, Miss Enid! Don't ask to do anything against the master.

ENID - How can you love him?

RODGERS - Love him! No, no, I don't love him, Miss Enid. But I fear him —oh! I fear him. One glance of his eyes seems to cut me—to pierce me like a sword. I wouldn't even listen to anything against him, for I feel it would come round to him, and then—then—!

ENID - What can he do to you?

RODGERS - Oh, I couldn't, Miss Enid—don't ask me. What a man! what a man! Has he a child in his room, Miss Enid?

ENID - A child?

RODGERS - Yes—the milk—who drinks the milk? He drinks no milk. Every morning I take up the jug of milk. And the music, who is it he plays the music to?

ENID - Music! You have heard it, too. I'm so frightened. I'm in danger. I know I'm in danger. (Rising.)

RODGERS - In danger, Miss Enid?

ENID - And you can save me.

RODGERS - Oh, Miss Enid, I couldn't—I couldn't—I have no nerve. I couldn't.

ENID - All I want you to do is to take a telegram.

RODGERS - A telegram, Miss Enid?

ENID - They won't let me out, and yet I must send it.

RODGERS - Perhaps they won't let me out.

ENID - You could wait a little, and then slip away to the office.

RODGERS - What is the telegram, Miss Enid? Say it slowly. My poor old head is not as clear as it used to be.

ENID - Give it to the clerk.

RODGERS - No, no, I must be sure it is nothing against the master.

ENID - It is my business—only mine. Your master's name is not even mentioned. See—it is to Mr. Sherlock Holmes—he is a friend of mine—Baker Street, London. "Come to me as soon as you can. Please hurry." That is All. Dear Rodgers, it means so much to me—please —please take it for me.

RODGERS - I can't understand things like I used.

ENID - Oh! do take it, Rodgers! You said yourself that I had always been kind to you. You will take it, won't you? (Holds out telegram to RODGERS.)

RODGERS - Yes, yes, I will take it, Miss Enid. (Takes telegram and puts it in his pocket.)

ENID - Oh! you don't know what a service you are doing. It may save me —it may save my going all the way to town.

RODGERS - Well, well, of course I will take it. What's that?

(Wheels heard outside.)

(Enter MRS. STAUNTON and ALI.)

MRS. STAUNTON - Quick, Ali! get the door unlocked. He won't like to be kept waiting. Rodgers, be ready to receive your master.

ENID - (to RODGERS) Don't forget—as soon as you can.

(She goes into the bedroom wing, followed by MRS. STAUNTON.)

(Wheels stop.)

(ALI throws open the hall door and salaams. Enter RYLOTT, followed by HOLMES, disguised as Peters, the new butler, who is followed by BILLY, disguised as a young girl, with a big hat-box.)

RYLOTT - (taking off things and handing them to ALI) Where is Miss Enid? Did she return?

ALI - Yes, sir, she is in her room.

RYLOTT - Ah! (To RODGERS) What! still here.

RODGERS - I had some hopes, sir—

RYLOTT - Get away! Lay the supper! I'll deal with you presently.

(RODGERS goes into the servants' hall.)

Ali, you can go also. Show this young girl to the kitchen. (To HOLMES.) What is her name?

HOLMES - Amelia—the same as her mother's.

RYLOTT - Go to the kitchen, child, and make yourself useful.

(ALI goes out, followed by BILLY.)

(To HOLMES.) Now, my man, we may as well understand each other first as last. I'm a man who stands no nonsense in my own house. I give good pay, but I exact good service. Do you understand?

HOLMES - Yes, sir.

RYLOTT - I've had a man for some time, but he is old and useless. I want a younger man to keep the place in order. Rodgers will show you the cellar and the other things you should know. You take over from to-morrow morning.

HOLMES - Very good, sir. I'm sure, sir, it was very good of you to take me with such an encumbrance as my poor little orphaned Amelia.

RYLOTT - I've taken you not only with a useless encumbrance but without references and without a character. Why have I done that? Because I expect I shall get better service out of you. Where are you to find a place if you lose this one? Don't you forget it.

HOLMES - I won't forget, sir. I'll do all I can. If I can speak to your late butler, sir, I have no doubt he will soon show me my duties.

RYLOTT - Very good. (Rings bell.)

(Enter MRS. STAUNTON from the bedroom wing.)

Mrs. Staunton, tell Rodgers I want him. By the way, where is Siva?

MRS. STAUNTON - Loose in the park, sir.

(She goes into the servants' hall.)

RYLOTT - By the way, I had best warn you, Peters, not to go out till my boar-hound comes to know you. She's not safe with strangers—not very safe with any one but myself.

HOLMES - I'll remember, sir.

RYLOTT - Warn that girl of yours.

(Enter RODGERS.)

HOLMES - Yes, I will.

RYLOTT - Ah, Rodgers, you will hand your keys over to Peters. When you have done so, come to me in the study.

RODGERS - Yes, sir.

(RYLOTT goes into his study.)

HOLMES - (after looking round) Well, I'm not so sure that I think so much of this place. Maybe you are the lucky one after all. I hope I am not doing you out of your job. I'd chuck it for two pins. If it wasn't for Amelia I'd chuck it now.

RODGERS - If it wasn't you it would be some one else. Old Rodgers is finished—used up. But he said he wanted to see me in the study. What do you think he wants with me in the study?

HOLMES - Maybe to thank you for your service; maybe to make you a parting present.

RODGERS - His eyes were hard as steel. What can he want with me? I get nervous these days, Mr. Peters. What was it he told me to do?

HOLMES - To hand over the keys. (Taking his overcoat off)

RODGERS - Yes, yes, the keys. (Taking out keys.) They are here, Mr. Peters. That's the cellar key, Mr. Peters. Be careful about the cellar. That was the first time he struck me—when I mistook the claret for the Burgundy. He's often hasty, but he always kept his hands off till then.

HOLMES - But the more I see of this place the less I fancy it. I'd be off to-night, but it's not so easy these days to get a place if your papers ain't in order. See here, Mr. Rodgers, I'd like to know a little more about my duties. The study is there, ain't it?

RODGERS - Yes, he is there now, waiting—waiting for me.

HOLMES - Where is his room?

RODGERS - You see the passage yonder. Well, the first room you come to is the master's bedroom; the next is Miss Enid's—

HOLMES - I see. Well, now, could you take me along to the master's room and show me any duties I have there?

RODGERS - The master's room? No one ever goes into the master's room. All the time I've been here I've never put my head inside the door.

HOLMES - (surprised) What? no one at all?

RODGERS - Ali goes. Ali is the Indian valet. But no one else.

HOLMES - I wonder you never mistook the door and just walked in.

RODGERS - You couldn't do that for the door is locked.

HOLMES - Oh! he locks his door does he? Dear me! None of the keys here any use, I suppose?

RODGERS - Don't think of such a thing. What are you saying? Why should you wish to enter the master's room?

HOLMES - I don't want to enter it. The fewer rooms the less work. Why do you suppose he locks the door?

RODGERS - It is not for me nor for you to ask why the master does things. He chooses to do so. That is enough for us.

HOLMES - Well Mr. Rodgers if you'll excuse my saying so, this old 'ouse 'as taken some of the spirit out of you. I'm sure I don't wonder. I don't see myself staying here very long. Wasn't there some one died here not so long ago?

RODGERS - I'd rather not talk of it, Mr. Peters.

HOLMES - A woman died in the room next the doctor's. The cabman was telling me as we drove up.

RODGERS - Don't listen to them, Mr. Peters. The master would not like it. Here is Miss Enid and the Doctor wants me.

(Enter ENID from the bedroom wing)

ENID - Rodgers can I have a word with you?

RODGERS - Very sorry Miss Enid, the master wants me.

(RODGERS goes into the study)

ENID - (to HOLMES) Are you—?

HOLMES - I am Peters, Miss, the new butler

ENID - Oh! (Sits down beside table and writes)

(HOLMES crosses and stands behind the table. Pause)

Why do you stand there? Are you a spy set to watch me? Am I never to have one moment of privacy?

HOLMES - I beg pardon, Miss.

ENID - I'm sorry if I have spoken bitterly. I have had enough to make me bitter.

HOLMES - I'm very sorry. Miss. I'm new to the place and don't quite know where I am yet. May I ask Miss if your name is Stonor?

ENID - Yes. Why do you ask?

HOLMES - There was a lad at the station with a message for you.

ENID - (rising) A message for me! Oh! it is what I want of All things on earth! Why did you not take it?

HOLMES - I did take it, Miss, it is here. (Hands her a note.)

ENID - (tears it open, reads) "Fear nothing, and stay where you are. All will be right. Holmes." Oh! it is a ray of sunshine in the darkness —such darkness. Tell me, Peters, who was this boy?

HOLMES - I don't know, Miss—just a very ordinary nipper. The Doctor had gone on to the cab, and the boy touched my sleeve and asked me to give you this note in your own hand.

ENID - You said nothing to the Doctor.

HOLMES - Well, Miss, it seemed to be your business, not his. I just took it, and there it is.

ENID - God bless you for it. (She conceals the note in her bosom.)

HOLMES - I'm only a servant, Miss, but if I can be of any help to you, you must let me know.

(HOLMES goes into the bedroom wing.)

(ENID takes the note out of her bosom, reads it again, then hurriedly replaces it as RYLOTT and RODGERS re-enter.)

RYLOTT - Very good. You can go and pack your box.

RODGERS - (cringing) Yes, sir. You won't—

RYLOTT - That's enough. Get away!

(RODGERS goes into the servants' hall.)

(ENID sits at the tea-table.)

(Comes over to ENID.) There you are! I want a word or two with you. What the devil do you mean by slipping off to London the moment my back was turned? And what did you do when you got there?

ENID - I went there on my own business.

RYLOTT - Oh! on your own business, was it? Perhaps what you call your own business may prove to be my business also. Who did you see? Come, woman, tell me!

ENID - It was my own business. I am of age. You have no claim to control me.

RYLOTT - I know exactly where you went. You went to the rooms of Mr. Sherlock Holmes, where you met Dr. Watson, who had advised you to go there. Was it not so?

ENID - I will answer no questions. If I did as you say, I was within my rights.

RYLOTT - What have you been saying about me? What did you go to consult Mr. Holmes about?

(ENID remains silent)

D'you hear? What did you go about? By God, I'll find a way to make you speak! (Seizes her by the arm.) Come!

(Enter HOLMES)

HOLMES - Yes, sir?

RYLOTT - I did not ring for you.

HOLMES - I thought you called.

RYLOTT - Get out of this! What do you mean?

HOLMES - I beg your pardon, sir.

(He goes into the servants hall.)

(RYLOTT goes to the door of the servants hall, looks through, then returns.)

RYLOTT - Look here Enid, let us be sensible. I was too hot now. But you must realize the situation. Your wisest and safest course is complete submission. If you do what I tell you, there be no friction between us.

ENID - What do you wish me to do?

RYLOTT - Your marriage will complicate the arrangement which was come to at your mother's death. I want you of own free will to bind yourself to respect it. Come Enid, you would not wish that your happiness should cause loss and even penury to me. I am an elderly man. I have had losses too, which make it the more necessary that I should preserve what is left. If you will sign a little deed it will be best for both of us.

ENID - I have promised to sign nothing until a lawyer has seen it.

RYLOTT - Promised? Promised whom?

ENID - I promised my fiancée.

RYLOTT - Oh! you did, did you? But why should lawyers come between you and me, Enid? I beg you—I urge you to do what I ask (Opening out papers before her.)

ENID - No, no. I cannot. I will not.

RYLOTT - Very good! Tell me the truth, Enid. I won't be angry. What are your suspicions of me?

ENID - I have no suspicions.

RYLOTT - Did I not receive your fiancé with civility?

ENID - Yes, you did.

RYLOTT - Have I not, on the whole, been kind to you all this winter?

ENID - Yes, you have.

RYLOTT - Then, tell me, child, why do you suspect me?

ENID - I don't suspect you.

RYLOTT - Why do you send out messages to get help against me?

ENID - I don't understand you.

RYLOTT - Don't you send out for help? Tell me the truth, child.

ENID - No.

RYLOTT - (with a yell) You damned little liar! (Bangs the telegram down before her.) What was this telegram that you gave to Rodgers?

(ENID sinks back, half fainting.)

Ah! you infernal young hypocrite. Shall I read it to you? "Come to me as soon as you can. Please hurry." What did you mean by that? What did you mean, I say? (Clutching her arm.) None of your lies—out with it.

ENID - Keep your hands off me, you coward!

RYLOTT - Answer me—answer me, then!

ENID - I will answer you! I believe that you murdered my mother by your neglect. I believe that in some way you drove my sister to her grave. Now, I am certain that you mean to do the same to me. You're a murderer—a murderer! We were left to your care—helpless girls. You have ill-used us—you have tortured us—now you have murdered one of us, and you would do the same to me. You are a coward, a monster, a man fit only for the gallows!

RYLOTT - You'll pay for this, you little devil! Get to your room.

ENID - I will. I'm not without friends, as you may find.

RYLOTT - You've got some plot against me. What have you been arranging in London? What is it? (Clutches her.)

ENID - Let me go!

RYLOTT - What did you tell them? By God, I'll twist your head off your shoulders if you cross me! (Seizes her by the neck.)

ENID - Help! Help!

(Enter HOLMES.)

HOLMES - Hands off, Dr. Rylott.

(RYLOTT releases ENID.)

You had best go to your room, young lady. I'll see that you are not molested. Go at once, I tell you, go.

RYLOTT - You infernal villain. I'll soon settle you.

(After ENID goes out, he runs to a rack at the side, gets a whip, opens the hall door, stands near it with his whip.)

Now, then, out you go! By George, you'll remember Stoke Moran.

HOLMES - Excuse me, sir, but is that a whip?

RYLOTT - You'll soon see what it is.

HOLMES - I am afraid I must ask you to put it down.

RYLOTT - Oh, indeed! must you? (Comes forward to him.)

HOLMES - (taking out a revolver) Yes, sir! You'll please put down that whip.

RYLOTT - (falling back) You villain!

HOLMES - Stand right back, sir. I'll take no risks with a man like you. Right back, I say! Thank you, sir.

RYLOTT - Rodgers! Ali! My gun!

(He runs into his study.)

HOLMES - Hurry up, Billy! No time to lose.

(Enter BILLY, as Amelia, from the servants' hall.)

BILLY - Yes, Mr. Holmes.

(HOLMES and BILLY go out through the entrance hall.)

(Several shots are heard outside. RYLOTT rushes in from his study with his gun.)

(Enter ALI—running in from outside.)

ALI - Stop, Sahib, stop!

RYLOTT - What were those shots?

ALI - The new butler, sir. He shoot Siva!

RYLOTT - Shot my dog! By God, I'll teach him! (Rushes toward door.)

ALI - No, no, Sahib. He gone in darkness. What do you do? People come. Police come.

RYLOTT - You're right. (Puts gun down.) We have another game; Ali, you will watch outside Miss Enid's window to-night.

ALI - Yes, Sahib, shall I watch all night?

RYLOTT - All night? No, not all night! You will learn when you may cease your watch.

CURTAIN

SCENE 2. Enid's Bedroom, Stoke Place

ENID is discovered seated near the lamp at a small table near a window. A knock is heard at the door

ENID - Who is there?

RYLOTT - (off) It is I.

ENID - What do you want?

RYLOTT - Why is your light still burning?

ENID - I have been reading.

RYLOTT - You are not in bed then?

ENID - Not yet.

RYLOTT - Then I desire to come in.

ENID - But it is so late.

RYLOTT - (rattles door) Come, come, let me in this instant.

ENID - No, no I cannot!

RYLOTT - Must I break the door in?

ENID - I will open it. I will open it. (Opens door.) Why do persecute me so?

(RYLOTT enters in his dressing gown.)

RYLOTT - Why are you so childish and so suspicious? Your mind has brooded upon your poor sister's death until you have built up these fantastic suspicions against me. Tell me now Enid—I'm not such a bad sort you know, if you only deal frankly with me. Tell me, have you any idea of your own about how your sister died? Was that what you went to Mr. Holmes about this morning? Couldn't you take me into your confidence as well as him? Is it not natural that I should feel hurt when I see you turn to a stranger for advice?

ENID - How my poor sister met her death only your own wicked heart can know. I am as sure that it came to her through you as if I had seen you strike her down. You may kill me if you like, but I will tell you what I think.

RYLOTT - My dear child, you are overwrought and hysterical. What can have put such wild ideas into your head? After all, I may have a hasty temper —I have often deplored it to you—but what excuse have I ever given you for such monstrous suspicions?

ENID - You think that by a few smooth words you can make me forget all your past looks, your acts. You cannot deceive me, I know the danger and I face it.

RYLOTT - What, then, is the danger?

ENID - It is near me to-night, whatever it is.

RYLOTT - Why do you think so?

ENID - Why is that Indian watching in the darkness? I opened my window just now, and there he was. Why is he there?

RYLOTT - To prevent your making a public fool of yourself. You are capable of getting loose and making a scandal.

ENID - He is there to keep me in my room until you come to murder me.

RYLOTT - Upon my word, I think your brain is unhinged. Now, look here, Enid, be reasonable for a moment.

ENID - What's that?

RYLOTT - What is it, then?

ENID - I thought I heard a cry.

RYLOTT - It's the howling of the wind. Listen to me. If there is friction between us—and I don't for a moment deny that there is—why is it? You think I mean to hurt you. I could only have one possible motive for hurting you. Why not remove that motive? Then you could no longer work yourself into these terrors. Here is that legal paper I spoke of. Mrs. Staunton could witness it. All I want is your signature.

ENID - No, never.

RYLOTT - Never!

ENID - Unless my lawyer advises it.

RYLOTT - Is that final?

ENID - (springing up) Yes, it is. I will never sign it.

RYLOTT - Well, I have done my best for you. It was your last chance.

ENID - Ah! then you do mean murder.

RYLOTT - The last chance of regaining my favour. You – (Pause.) Get to your bed and may you wake in a more rational mood to- morrow. You will not be permitted to make a scandal. Ali will be at his post outside, and I shall sit in the hall; so you may reconcile yourself to being quiet. Nothing more to say to me?

(He goes out.)

(When he has gone, ENID listens to his departing footsteps. Then she locks the door once again, and looks round her.)

ENID - What is that tapping? Surely I heard tapping! Perhaps it is the pulse within my own brain?

(Tapping.)

Yes! there it is again! Where was it? Is it the signal of death? (Looks wildly round the walls.) Ah! it grows louder. It is the window. (Goes towards window.) A man! a man crouching in the darkness. Still tapping. It's not Ali! The face was white. Ah!

(The window opens and HOLMES enters.)

HOLMES - My dear young lady, I trust that I don't intrude.

ENID - Oh, Mr. Holmes, I'm so glad to see you! Save me! save me! Mr. Holmes, they mean to murder me.

HOLMES - Tut, tut! We mean that they shall do nothing of sort.

ENID - I had given up all hope of your coming.

HOLMES - These old-fashioned window-catches are most inefficient.

ENID - How did you pass the Indian and the dog?

HOLMES - Well, as to the Indian, we chloroformed him. Watson is busy tying him up in the arbour at the present moment. The dog I was compelled to shoot at an earlier stage of the proceeding.

ENID - You shot Siva!

HOLMES - I might have been forced to shoot her master also. It was after I sent you to your room. He threatened me with a whip.

ENID - You were—you were Peters, the butler.

HOLMES - (feeling the walls) I wanted to be near you. So this is the famous room, is it? Dear me! very much as I had pictured it. You will excuse me for not discovering myself to you, but any cry or agitation upon your part would have betrayed me.

ENID - But your daughter Amelia?

HOLMES - Ah, yes, I take Billy when I can. Billy as messenger is invaluable.

ENID - Then you intended to watch over me till night?

HOLMES - Exactly. But the man's brutality caused me to show my hand too soon. However, I have never been far from your window. I gather the matter is pressing.

ENID - He means to murder me to-night.

HOLMES - He is certainly in an ugly humour. He is not in his room at present.

ENID - No, he is in the hall.

HOLMES - So we can talk with safety. What has become of the excellent Watson? (Approaches window.) Come in, Watson, come in!

(Enter WATSON from window.)

How is our Indian friend?

WATSON - He is coming out of the chloroform; but he can neither move nor speak. Good evening, Miss Stonor, what a night it is.

ENID - How can I thank you for coming?

HOLMES - You'll find Dr. Watson a useful companion on such an occasion. He has a natural turn for violence—some survival of his surgical training. The wind is good. Its howling will cover all sounds. Just sit in the window, Watson, and see that our retreat is safe. With your leave, I will inspect the room a little more closely. Now, my dear young lady, I can see that you are frightened to death, and no wonder. Your courage, so far, has been admirable. Sit over here by the fire.

ENID - If he should come—!

HOLMES - In that case answer him. Say that you have gone to bed. (Takes lamp from table.) A most interesting old room—very quaint indeed! Old-fashioned comfort without modern luxury. The passage is, as I understand, immediately outside?

ENID - Yes.

HOLMES - Mr. Peters made two attempts to explore the ground, but without avail. By the way, I gather that you tried to send me a message, and that old Rodgers gave it to your stepfather.

ENID - Yes, he did.

HOLMES - He is not to be blamed. His master controls him. He had to betray you. (Placing lamp down.)

ENID - It was my fault.

HOLMES - Well, well, it was an indiscretion, but it didn't matter. Let me see now, on this side is the room under repair. Quite so. Only one door. This leads into the passage?

ENID - Yes.

HOLMES - And that passage to the hall?

ENID - Yes.

HOLMES - Here is where the genial old gentleman sleeps when he is so innocently employed. Where is his door?

ENID - Down the passage.

HOLMES - Surely I heard him—(A step is heard in the passage.)

ENID - Yes, it's his step.

(HOLMES holds his hat over the light. There is a knock at the door.)

RYLOTT - (outside door) Enid!

ENID - What is it?

RYLOTT - Are you in bed?

ENID - Yes.

RYLOTT - Are you still of the same mind?

ENID - Yes, I am.

(Pause. They all listen.)

HOLMES (whispering): Has he gone into his room?

ENID - (crossing to door, listening) No, he's gone down the passage again to the hall.

HOLMES - Then we must make the most of the time. Might I trouble you, Watson, for the gimlet and the yard measure? Thank you! The lantern also. Thank you! You can turn up the lamp. I am interested in this partition wall. (Standing on the bed.) No little surprise, I suppose? No trap- doors and sliding panels? Funny folk, our ancestors, with a quaint taste in practical joking. (Gets on bed and fingers the wall.) No, it seems solid enough. Dear me! and yet you say your sister fastened both door and window. Remarkable. My lens, Watson. A perfectly respectable wall—in fact, a commonplace wall. Trap-door in the floor? (Kneels at one side of the bed, then the other.) No, nothing suspicious in that direction. Ancient carpeting—(crossing round bed)—oak wainscot — nothing more. Hullo! (Pulling at bed- post.)

WATSON - Why, what is it?

HOLMES - Why is your bed clamped to the floor?

ENID - I really don't know.

HOLMES - Was the bed in your other room clamped?

ENID - No, I don't think it was.

HOLMES - Very interesting. Most interesting and instructive. And this bell- pull—where does it communicate with?

ENID - It does not work.

HOLMES - But if you want to ring?

ENID - There is another over here.

HOLMES - Then why this one?

ENID - I don't know. There were some changes after we came here.

HOLMES - Quite a burst of activity, apparently. It took some strange shapes. (Standing on the bed.) You may be interested to know that the bell-rope ends in a brass hook. No wire attachment; it is a dummy. Dear me! how very singular. I see a small screen above it, which covers a ventilator, I suppose?

ENID - Yes, Mr. Holmes, there is a ventilator.

HOLMES - Curious fad to ventilate one room into another when one could as well get the open air. Most original man, the architect. Very singular indeed. There is no means of opening the flap from here; it must open on the other side.

WATSON - What do you make of it, Holmes?

HOLMES - Suggestive, my dear Watson, very suggestive. Might I trouble you for your knife? With your permission, Miss Stonor, I will make a slight alteration. (Stands on bed-head and cuts the bell-pull.)

WATSON - Why do you do that, Holmes?

HOLMES - Dangerous, Watson, dangerous. Bear in mind that this opening, concealed by a flap of wood, leads into the room of our cheery Anglo-Indian neighbour. I repeat the adjective, Watson—Anglo- Indian.

WATSON - Well, Holmes?

HOLMES - The bed is clamped so that it cannot be shifted. He has a dummy bell- pull which leads to the bed. He has a hole above it which opens on his room. He is an Anglo-Indian doctor. Do you make nothing of all this? The music, too? The music. What is the music?

WATSON - A signal, Holmes.

HOLMES - A signal! A signal to whom?

WATSON - An accomplice.

HOLMES - Exactly. An accomplice who could enter a room with locked doors —an accomplice who could give a sure death which leaves no trace. An accomplice who can only be attracted back by music.

ENID - Hush! he is gone to his room.

(A door is heard to close outside.)

Listen! The door is shut.

HOLMES - (as Watson is about to take up lamp) Keep the lamp covered, so that if the ventilator is opened no light will show. He must think the girl is asleep. Keep the dark lantern handy. We must wait in the dark. I fancy we shall not have long to wait.

ENID - I am so frightened.

HOLMES - It is too much for you.

WATSON - Can I do anything, Holmes?

HOLMES - You can hand me my hunting-crop. Hush! What's that?

(Flute music is heard.)

My stick, Watson—quick, be quick! Now take the lantern. Have you got it? When I cry, "Now!" turn it full blaze upon the top of the bell- rope. Do you understand?

WATSON - Yes.

HOLMES - Down that bell-rope comes the messenger of death. It guides to the girl's pillow. Hush! the flap!

(The flap opens, disclosing a small square of light. This light is obscured. Music a good deal louder.)

(Cries sharply.) Now!

(WATSON turns the lantern full on to the bell-rope. A snake is half through the hole. HOLMES lashes at it with his stick. It disappears backwards.)

(The flute music stops.)

WATSON - It has gone.

HOLMES - Yes, it has gone, but we know the truth.

(A loud cry is heard.)

WATSON - What is that?

HOLMES - I believe the devil has turned on its master.

(Another cry.)

It is in the passage. (Throws open the door.)

(In the doorway is seen DR. RYLOTT in shirt and trousers, the snake round his head and neck.)

RYLOTT - Save me! Save me!

(RYLOTT rushes in and falls on the floor. WATSON strikes at the snake as it writhes across the room.)

WATSON - (looking at the snake) The brute is dead.

HOLMES - (looking at RYLOTT) So is the other.

(They both run to support the fainting lady.)

HOLMES - Miss Stonor, there is no more danger for you under this roof.

CURTAIN

Arthur Conan Doyle - A Short Biography

The Scottish physician and writer Sir Arthur Ignatius Conan Doyle's name is inseparable from the phenomenon of Sherlock Holmes, undoubtedly his greatest character and the eponymous meticulous, deductive and frankly genius hero of crime fiction. However, his prolific writing was in more than just the crime fiction genre; alongside the 56 short stories and 4 novels of Sherlock Holmes he explored science fiction and fantasy as well as plays, historical novels and poetry. Another of Conan Doyle's notable characters is Professor Challenger, whose aggression and dominance serves as the antithesis of Holmes, and demonstrates Conan Doyle's capacious imagination and dramatic skill. Returning to his name, it is worthy of note that there is uncertainty surrounding his surname; while he is often referred to as Conan Doyle, where Conan and Doyle are treated as a compound surname, the entry at his baptism records Arthur Ignatius Conan as first names, and Doyle as a solitary last. Indeed, his father's name was simply Doyle. Moreover, the catalogues of the British Library and the Library of Congress insist of Doyle as his surname. Regardless, he began to refer to himself as Conan Doyle and his second wife would take this as her surname, so he will herein be referred to as Conan Doyle, in accordance with his apparent preference.

He was born in Edinburgh at 11 Picardy Place on 22nd May 1859 to his parents Charles Altamont Doyle, an Englishman of Irish descent, and Mary (née Foley), an Irishwoman, who had married in 1855. He had a brother named Innes. Charles was developing an alcohol dependence which would become incompatible with family life, and they dispersed in 1864 at which point the children were temporarily housed at various addresses across Edinburgh. They reunited in 1867, only to live together at 3 Sciennes place in a squalid tenement flat. Fortunately for the children, they had wealthy uncles who were willing to support them by paying for education and clothing. Accordingly at the age of nine Conan Doyle was sent to Hodder Place, Stonyhurst, a Roman Catholic Jesuit preparatory school. He was here for the two years between 1868 and 1870 at which point he went on to Stonyhurst College where he stayed until 1875 when he went for a year to Stella Matutina, Jesuit school in Feldkirch, Austria.

This school education set him up for a place at the University of Edinburgh, where he studied medicine between 1876 and 1881. Part of his course involved placements in Aston, (now a suburb of Birmingham, though at the time it was its own town), Sheffield and in Ruyton-XI-Towns, an unusually named village in Shropshire which acquired its numeral when, in the twelfth century, a castle was built there which became the focus of eleven small and disparate communities. It was during this study that he began writing short stories, with the successful submission of 'The Haunted Grange of Goresthorpe' to Blackwood's Magazine arguably his greatest literary achievement at the time. As well as this recognition, he saw his first published piece 'The Mystery of the Sasassa Valley', a story set in South Africa, printed on 6th September 1879 in Chambers's Edinburgh Journal, and only 17 days later his first non-fiction article was published in the British Medical Journal on 20th September, entitled 'Gelsemium as poison'. Having finished his studies he took an appointment as a Doctor on the Greenland whaler Hope of Peterhead in 1880 and then, following his graduation, he assumed the role of ship's surgeon on the SS Mayumba during its 1881 voyage to the West African coast.

1882 saw his move to Plymouth where he joined the medical practice of former classmate George Turnavine Budd, though they had a difficult professional relationship and Conan Doyle left shortly thereafter in order to set up his own independent practice. Having arrived in Portsmouth in June of that year and disembarked the SS Mayumba with a mere £10 (£700 today) to his name, he proceeded to establish his practice at 1 Bush Billas in Elm Grove, Southsea, a seaside town in the country of Hampshire. He was not met with initial success, and in order to pass the time between visits from patients he resumed his story writing. During this period he completed his first novel, The Mystery of Cloomber, though it was not published until 1888, and the unfinished Narrative of John Smith, which only recently saw publication in 2011. Alongside these longer works was the steady production of a portfolio of short stories which included 'The Captain of the Pole-Star' and 'J. Habakuk Jephson's Statement', both inspired by the time he spent at sea. Meanwhile, in 1885 he completed a doctorate on the subject of tabes dorsalis, the slow degradation and demyelination of the sensory neurons that carry afferent information. He also married Louisa Hawkins, who was the sister of one of his patients, that same year. However, two years after this marriage he met and fell in love with Jean Elizabeth Leckie, though he maintained a platonic relationship with her out of respect for and loyalty to his wife for whom he still had great affection.

Though he struggled to find a publisher for the stories he wrote in these stretches of inactivity, his literary career would take an historic turn in 1886 when, on 20th November, Ward Lock & Co offered Conan Doyle £25 for all rights to A Study In Scarlet. The first and one of the most famous of the Sherlock Holmes franchise, it introduced the public to a new, empirical and methodical mode of crime fiction, and indeed criminality itself, by the combination of a perspicacious, brilliantly observant and data-driven detective whose army doctor companion Watson provided further scientific support as well as a means of observing and narrating Holmes's processes and adventures. The novel was a success; a letter from Robert Louis Stevenson who had acquired a copy of the novel in Samoa, wrote with "[his] compliments on your very ingenious very interesting adventures of Sherlock Holmes", while noting the similarity between Holmes's methods and a certain Joseph Bell, upon whom Holmes was based. Conan Doyle even wrote to Bell explaining so, and that "round the centre of deduction and inference and observation which I have heard you inculcate I have tried to build up a man". It was met with positive reviews in The Scotsman and The Herald and this success encouraged Ward Lock & Co to commission a sequel, The Sign of Four, which appeared in Lippincott's Magazine in February 1890, under agreement with the Ward Lock company. On 28th January 1889 his first child was born, Mary Louise, and three years later on 15th November 1892 they had a boy, Arthur Alleyne Kingsley, who became known only as Kingsley.

Now that he had a family to look after, he began to look more closely at the arrangement he had with his publishers and Conan Doyle soon began to feel that, as a new, inexperienced writer, he had been somewhat exploited by them, resolving to curtail his involvement with their business and instead beginning to write for the Strand Magazine from his home at 2 Wimpole Street. Meanwhile Conan Doyle was enjoying something of a sporting career, playing under the pseudonym A.C. Smith as goalkeeper for Portsmouth Association Football Club (though this club had no connection to present-day Portsmouth F.C, founded two years after Conan Doyle's amateur side disbanded in 1896). He was also a keen cricketer and played ten first-class matches between 1899 and 1907 for the Marylebone Cricket Club, making a highest score with the bat of 43 against London County. As an occasional bowler he only took one wicket in these ten matches, though it was W.G. Grace's stumps which he hit; a notable triumph of the right arm. His sporting interests extended to golf, for which he was elected captain of the Crowborough Beacon Golf Club in East Sussex for 1910. He once even visited Rudyard Kipling at his farm in America, bringing with him a set of golf clubs and giving his fellow famous writer an extended two-day lesson.

He went to Vienna to study ophthalmology in 1890 before returning to London and setting up a practice as an ophthalmologist, though he recorded in his autobiography that not a single patient ever crossed his doorway. This left him with more time for his writing, though by now he was beginning to feel somewhat exhausted by Holmes and wrote to his mother in 1891 "I think of slaying Holmes ... and winding him up for good and all. He takes my mind from better things." This was met with an entreaty from his mother of "you won't! You can't! You mustn't!" These "better things" were his historical novels such as The White Company (1891) and The Great Shadow (1892). Then, in defiance of his mother and the wishes of the general public, in December 1893 he wrote Holmes's apparent death in the clutches of a high-consequence brawl with arch-nemesis Moriarty above the Reichenbach Falls in Germany. Both of their deaths seemed certain, and it seemed the end of the Sherlock Holmes phenomenon. He now had time to focus on other work, most notably his pamphlet justifying the United Kingdom's involvement with the Boer War, an involvement for which they were frequently and heavily criticised. The War in South Africa: Its Cause and Conduct was widely translated after its publication in 1902, and was based to a certain extent on the time he had spent as a volunteer doctor in the Langman Field Hospital at Bloemfontein between March and June 1900. It was this and his book The Great Boer War, written in 1900, which he considered the reasons for his knighthood in 1902 by King Edward VII, and he was subsequently appointed Deputy-Lieutenant of Surrey. In 1903 however, owing to the public demand of which he became increasingly aware after successive letters from fans pleading for the resurrection of their great hero, he seemingly brought Holmes back from the dead; in 'The Adventure of the Empty House', the first story for ten years, he reassures the reader that Holmes had merely arranged for his fall to appear fatal in order that his other enemies (particularly Colonel Sebastian Moran) might consider him dead also, whereas in reality he never falls at all. Fans were ecstatic and Conan Doyle continued to write Holmes stories.

His interest in politics piqued by the issues surrounding the Boer War, the interest he had in criminal justice which was so prominent in his crime fiction transferred to that of real-life and he became a fervent advocate of justice, investigating two closed cases of incorrect conviction. The first, in 1906, saw the shy half-British, half- Indian lawyer George Edalji exonerated for imprisonment for crimes of mutilation towards animals which he hadn't committed. Though the police were convinced of their prosecution, the crimes continued even after he was imprisoned and Conan Doyle, analytical and methodical as his invention, proceeded to privately investigate the case and the outcome, Edalji's acquittal, encouraged the establishment of the Court of Criminal Appeal in 1907. Meanwhile his wife Louisa had been suffering from tuberculosis and died on the 4th July, and Conan Doyle married Jean Elizabeth Leckie, the woman with whom he had fallen in love in 1897, the year after. The second case of injustice was some twenty years later, though pertaining to a crime committed in 1908 allegedly by one Oscar Slater, a German Jew and gambling-den operator convicted of bludgeoning an 82 year old woman to death. Conan Doyle noticed inconsistencies in the evidence which, combined with his general sense of unease about the case, motivated him to pay for the majority of Slater's legal fees and eventually see him released in 1928.

He now had his first child with Jean, whom they named Denis Percy Stewart and was born on 17th March 1909, and then on 19th November 1910 they had Adrian Malcolm. Jean Lena Annette followed on 21st December 1912. Over the next few years there would be various deaths in his family. His first wife having already passed away, Kingsley was taken ill after complications of pneumonia following injury near the Somme in 1917. His two brothers-in-law also died, and after Kingsley's condition worsened and he passed away on 28th October owing to the complications of his convalescence and his brother Innes, now Brigadier-General died of the same, Conan Doyle sank into a deep depression, eventually finding solace in Christian spiritualism. Despite the veracity of his writing, he was not free from misunderstanding. Convinced of the authenticity of five (now known to be) hoaxed photographs of fairies by Elsie Wright in June 1917, he wrote a book The Coming of the Fairies in 1921 exploring them and other supernatural phenomena, followed up in 1926 by The History of Spiritualism, a broader look at the particulars of the movement. Encouraging the Spiritualists' National Union to modify their precepts, his turn to spiritualism was so strong that he wrote a Professor Challenger novel on the subject, entitled The Land of Mist, in 1926.

His friendship with Harry Houdini, another noted Spiritualist, led him to believe that Houdini was possessed of supernatural powers and that his feats were not tricks but proof of the supernatural. He expresses this view in The Edge of the Unknown (1930), and Houdini's inability to convince Conan Doyle of the illusory nature of his feats led to a bitter and very public falling-out. Conan Doyle has been posthumously implicated in the Piltdown Man hoax (and even accused of being its perpetrator by Richard Milner), a discovery of fossilised hominid remains which fooled the scientific world for over 40 years. Milner posits that Conan Doyle's motive was revenge on the scientific establishment for their debunking of Houdini, and that within The Lost World which was released the year the remains were found contains several hidden and encrypted clues indicating his involvement.

On 7th July 1930 Conan Doyle was discovered in the hall of Windlesham Manor, his house in Crowborough, East Sussex, clutching his chest. He died of a heart attack at the age of 71, and his last words, directed to his wife, were "you are wonderful". As a Spiritualist, his burial brought controversy as there was debate as to where he should properly be buried. Eventually he was interred on 11th July in Windlesham rose garden, though he was later removed and buried with his wife in Minstead churchyard in the New Forest, Hampshire.

The epitaph on that gravestone reads

Steel true
Blade straight
Arthur Conan Doyle
Knight
Patriot, Physician and man of letters

Arthur Conan Doyle - A Concise Bibliography

Periodical Publications

Title	Published On	Published In
"The Mystery of the Sasassa Valley"	October 1879	Chambers's Journal
"Gelseminum as a poison"	20 September 1879	British Medical Journal
"The American's Tale"	1879	London Society
"The Gully of Bluemansdyke"	1881	London Society
"Bones"	1882	London Society
"My Friend the Murderer"	1882	London Society
"J. Habakuk Jephson's Statement"	January 1884	Cornhill Magazine
"Life and Death in the Blood"	1884	Good Wordse
"Crabbe's Practice"	1884	The Boy's Own Paper
"The Fate of the Evangeline"	1885	The Boy's Own Paper

"A Psychologist's Wife"	1885	Blackwood's Magazine
"A Midshipman's Story"	December 1885	Cassell's Magazine
"Cyprian Overbeck Wells, or A Literary Mosaic"	1886	The Boy's Own Paper
"Uncle Jeremy's Household"	1887	The Boy's Own Paper
"The Stone of Boxman's Drift"	1887	The Boy's Own Paper
"An Exciting Christmas Eve"	1887	The Boy's Own Paper
"John Huxford's Hiatus"	June 1888	Cornhill Magazine
"The Geographical Distribution of British Intellect"	August 1888	The Nineteenth Century
"The Bravoes of Market Drayton"	August 1889	Chambers's Journal
"The Ring of Thoth"	January 1890	Cornhill Magazine
"The Surgeon of Gaster Fell"	December 1890	Chambers's Journal
"The Duello in France"	December 1890	Cornhill Magazine
"The White Company"	Jan –Dec 1891	Cornhill Magazine
"The Voice of Science"	March 1891	The Strand Magazine
"A Scandal in Bohemia"	July 1891	The Strand Magazine
"The Red-Headed League"	August 1891	The Strand Magazine
"A Case of Identity"	September 1891	The Strand Magazine
"The Boscombe Valley Mystery"	October 1891	The Strand Magazine
"The Five Orange Pips"	November 1891	The Strand Magazine
"The Man with the Twisted Lip"	December 1891	The Strand Magazine
"The Adventure of the Blue Carbuncle"	January 1892	The Strand Magazine
"The Adventure of the Speckled Band"	February 1892	The Strand Magazine
"The Adventure of the Engineer's Thumb"	March 1892	The Strand Magazine
"The Adventure of the Noble Bachelor"	April 1892	The Strand Magazine
"The Adventure of the Beryl Coronet"	May 1892	The Strand Magazine
"The Adventure of the Copper Beeches"	June 1892	The Strand Magazine
"A Day with Dr Conan Doyle"	August 1892	The Strand Magazine
"The Adventure of Silver Blaze"	December 1892	The Strand Magazine
"The Refugees"	January – June 1893	Harper's Magazine
"The Adventure of the Cardboard Box"	January 1893	The Strand Magazine
"The Adventure of the Yellow Face"	February 1893	The Strand Magazine
"The Adventure of the Stockbroker's Clerk"	March 1893	The Strand Magazine
"The Adventure of the Gloria Scott"	April 1893	The Strand Magazine
"The Adventure of the Musgrave Ritual"	May 1893	The Strand Magazine
"The Adventure of the Reigate Squire"	June 1893	The Strand Magazine
"The Green Flag"	June 1893	The Pall Mall Magazine
"The Adventure of the Crooked Man"	July 1893	The Strand Magazine
"The Adventure of the Resident Patient"	August 1893	The Strand Magazine
"Pennarby Mine"	August 1893	The Pall Mall Magazine
"The Adventure of the Greek Interpreter"	September 1893	The Strand Magazine
"The Adventure of the Naval Treaty"	Oct – Nov 1893	The Strand Magazine
"The Adventure of the Final Problem"	December 1893	The Strand Magazine
"The Stark Munro Letters"	1894–1895	The Idler
"The Lord of Chateau Noir"	July 1894	The Strand Magazine
"The Medal of Brigadier Gerard"	December 1894	The Strand Magazine
"The Alpine Pass on Ski"	December 1894	The Strand Magazine
"How the Brigadier Held the King"	April 1895	The Strand Magazine
"How the King Held the Brigadier"	May 1895	The Strand Magazine
"How the Brigadier Slew the Brothers of Ajaccio"	June 1895	The Strand Magazine
"How the Brigadier Came to the Castle of Gloom"	July 1895	The Strand Magazine
"How the Brigadier Took the Field Against the Marshal Millefleurs"	Aug 1895	The Strand Magazine
"How the Brigadier was Tempted by the Devil"	Sept 1895	The Strand Magazine
"How the Brigadier Played for a Kingdom"	December 1895	The Strand Magazine
"Rodney Stone"	Jan – Dec 1896	The Strand Magazine
"The Debut of Bombashi Joyce"	January 1897	Punch
"The Life on a Greenland Whaler"	January – June 1897	The Strand Magazine
"Uncle Barnac"	January – March 1897	The Queen

"The Tragedy of the Korosko"	May – December 1897	The Strand Magazine
"Cremona"	January 1898	Cornhill Magazine
"The Groom's Story"	April 1898	Cornhill Magazine
"The Story of the Beetle Hunter"	June 1898	The Strand Magazine
"The Story of the Man With the Watches"	July 1898	The Strand Magazine
"The Story of the Lost Special"	August 1898	The Strand Magazine
"The Story of the Sealed Room"	September 1898	The Strand Magazine
"The Story of the Black Doctor"	October 1898	The Strand Magazine
"The Story of the Club-Footed Grocer"	November 1898	The Strand Magazine
"The Story of the Brazilian Cat"	December 1898	The Strand Magazine
"The Story of the Japanned Box"	January 1899	The Strand Magazine
"The Story of the Jew's Breast-Plate"	February 1899	The Strand Magazine
"The Story of B.24"	March 1899	The Strand Magazine
"The Story of the Latin Tutor"	April 1899	The Strand Magazine
"The Story of the Brown Hand"	May 1899	The Strand Magazine
"The Croxley Master"	Oct – Dec 1899	The Strand Magazine
"The Crime of the Brigadier"	January 1900	The Strand Magazine
"Hilda Wade, 11"	January 1900	The Strand Magazine
"Hilda Wade, 12"	February 1900	The Strand Magazine
"Playing with Fire"	March 1900	The Strand Magazine
"A Glimpse of the Army"	September 1900	The Strand Magazine
"Some Military Lessons of the War"	October 1900	Cornhill Magazine
"The Military Lessons of the War, a Rejoinder"	January 1901	Cornhill Magazine
"The Holocaust of Manor Place"	March 1901	The Strand Magazine
"The Love Affair of George Vincent Parker"	April 1901	The Strand Magazine
"The Debatable Case of Mrs Emsley"	May 1901	The Strand Magazine
"A British Commando"	June 1901	The Strand Magazine
"The Hound of the Baskervilles"	Aug 1901 – April 1902	The Strand Magazine
"How Brigadier Gerard Lost an Ear"	August	The Strand Magazine
"How the Brigadier Saved the Army"	November 1902	The Strand Magazine
"How the Brigadier Rose to Minsk"	December 1902	The Strand Magazine
"Brigadier Gerard at Waterloo"	Jan – Feb 1903	The Strand Magazine
"The Brigadier in England"	March 1903	The Strand Magazine
"How the Brigidier Joined the Hussars at Conflans"	April 1903	The Strand Magazine
"How Etienne Gerard Said Goodbye to his Master"	May 1903	The Strand Magazine
"The Leather Funnel"	June 1903	The Strand Magazine
"The Adventure of the Empty House"	October 1903	The Strand Magazine
"The Adventure of the Norwood Builder"	November 1903	The Strand Magazine
"The Adventure of the Dancing Men"	December 1903	The Strand Magazine
"The Adventure of the Solitary Cyclist"	January 1904	The Strand Magazine
"The Adventure of the Priory School"	February 1904	The Strand Magazine
"The Adventure of Black Peter"	March 1904	The Strand Magazine
"The Adventure of Charles Augustus Milverton"	April 1904	The Strand Magazine
"The Adventure of the Six Napoleons"	May 1904	The Strand Magazine
"The Adventure of the Three Students"	June 1904	The Strand Magazine
"The Adventure of the Golden Pince-Nez"	July 1904	The Strand Magazine
"The Adventure of the Missing Three-Quarter"	August 1904	The Strand Magazine
"The Adventure of the Abbey Grange"	September 1904	The Strand Magazine
"The Adventure of the Second Stain"	December 1904	The Strand Magazine
"The Great Brown-Pericord Motor"	January 1905	The Pictorial Magazine
"Sir Nigel"	Dec 1905 – Dec 1906	The Strand Magazine
"An Incusion into Diplomacy"	June 1906	Cornhill Magazine
"Through the Magic Door"	Nov 1906 – Oct 1907	Cassell's Magazine
"The Pot of Caviare"	March 1908	The Strand Magazine
"The Silver Mirror"	August 1908	The Strand Magazine
"The Singular Experience of Mr. John Scott Eccles"	Sept 1908	The Strand Magazine
"The Tiger of San Pedro"	October 1908	The Strand Magazine

"The Adventure of the Bruce-Partington Plans"	December 1908	The Strand Magazine
"Shakespeare's Expostulation"	March 1909	Cornhill Magazine
"Bendy's Sermon"	April 1909	The Strand Magazine
"The Lord of Falcolnbridge"	August 1909	The Strand Magazine
"Some Recollections of Sport"	September 1909	The Strand Magazine
"The Homecoming"	December 1909	The Strand Magazine
"The Terror of Blue John Gap"	August 1910	The Strand Magazine
"The Marriage of the Brigadier"	September 1910	The Strand Magazine
"The Adventure of the Devil's Foot"	December 1910	The Strand Magazine
"The Adventure of the Red Circle"	March – April 1911	The Strand Magazine
"The Giant Maximin"	July 1911	The Literary Pageant
"One Crowded Hour"	August 1911	The Strand Magazine
"What Reform is Needed?"	September 1911	The Strand Magazine
"The Disappearance of Lady Frances Carfax"	December 1911	The Strand Magazine
"The Lost World"	April – Nov 1912	The Strand Magazine
"The Fall of Lord Barrymore"	December 1912	The Strand Magazine
"The Poison Belt"	March – July 1913	The Strand Magazine
"England and the Next War"	1913	The Fortnightly Review
"How it Happened"	September 1913	The Strand Magazine
"The Horror of the Heights"	November 1913	The Strand Magazine
"The Adventure of the Dying Detective"	December 1913	The Strand Magazine
"Essays Upon Phases of the Great War"	1914	The Fortnightly Review
"Danger!"	July 1914	The Strand Magazine
"The Valley of Fear"	Sept 1914 – May 1915	The Strand Magazine
"Western Wanderings"	January – April 1915	Cornhill Magazine
"Sherlock Holmes Drawn by a Typewriter"	August 1915	The Strand Magazine
"An Outing in War Time"	October 1915	The Strand Magazine
"Stranger than Fiction"	December 1915	The Strand Magazine
"The Prisoner's Defence"	February 1916	The Strand Magazine
"The British Campaign in France"	April – June 1917	The Strand Magazine
"Is Sir Oliver Lodge Right that the Dead Can Communicate?"	July 1917	The Strand Magazine
"What Will England be Like in 1930?"	August 1917	The Strand Magazine
"His Last Bow"	September 1917	The Strand Magazine
"Some Personalia about Mr Sherlock Holmes"	December 1917	The Strand Magazine
"Three of Them"	April 1918	The Strand Magazine
"The Battle of the Somme"	May – June 1918	The Strand Magazine
"Three of Them"	July – August 1918	The Strand Magazine
"The British Campaign in France"	Oct – Nov 1918	The Strand Magazine
"Three of Them"	December 1918	The Strand Magazine
"The Battle of Cambrai"	Jan – Feb 1919	The Strand Magazine
"Life After Death"	March 1919	The Strand Magazine
"The Uncharted Coast"	Dec 1919, Jan, May, Sept & Nov 1920	The Strand Magazine
"The Sideric Pendulum"	August 1920	The Strand Magazine
"Faries Photographed"	December 1920	The Strand Magazine
"The Evidence for Faries"	March 1921	The Strand Magazine
"The Uncharted Coast"	May 1921	The Strand Magazine
"Sherlock Holmes on the Film"	July 1921	The Strand Magazine
"The Adventure of the Mazarin Stone"	October 1921	The Strand Magazine
"The Bully of Brocas"	November 1921	The Strand Magazine
"The Nightmare Room"	December 1921	The Strand Magazine
"The Problem of Thor Bridge"	Feb – March 1922	The Strand Magazine
"The Lift"	June 1922	The Strand Magazine
"Now, Then Smith!"	July 1922	The Strand Magazine
"Sherlock Holmes in Real Life"	September 1922	The Strand Magazine
"A Point of Contact"	October 1922	The Story-Teller
"Billy's Bones"	December 1922	The Strand Magazine
"The Centurion"	December 1922	The Story-Teller

"The Cottingley Faries"	February 1923	The Strand Magazine
"The Adventure of the Creeping Man"	March 1923	The Strand Magazine
"Haunting Dreams"	April 1923	The Strand Magazine
"The Forbidden Subject"	August 1923	The Strand Magazine
"Memories and Adventures"	Oct 1923 – July 1924	The Strand Magazine
"How Our Novelists Write Their Books"	December 1924	The Strand Magazine
"The Adventure of the Three Garridebs"	January 1925	The Strand Magazine
"The Adventure of the Illustrious Client"	Feb –March 1925	The Strand Magazine
"The Land of Mist"	July 1925 – March 1926	The Strand Magazine
"The Adventure of the Three Gables"	October 1926	The Strand Magazine
"The Adventure of the Blanched Soldier"	November 1926	The Strand Magazine
"The Adventure of the Lion's Mane"	December 1926	The Strand Magazine
"The Adventure of the Retired Colourman"	January 1927	The Strand Magazine
"The Adventure of the Veiled Lodger"	February 1927	The Strand Magazine
"The Adventure of Shoscombe Old Place"	April 1927	The Strand Magazine
"W.G. Grace—A Memory"	July 1927	The Strand Magazine
"Houdini the Enigma"	August – Sept 1927	The Strand Magazine
"The Maracot Deep"	Oct 1927 – Feb 1928	The Strand Magazine
" When the World Screamed"	April – May 1928	The Strand Magazine
"The Dreamers—Notes from a Strange Mail Bag"	June 1928	The Strand Magazine
"The Story of Spedegue's Dropper"	October 1928	The Strand Magazine
"The Disintegration Machine"	January 1929	The Strand Magazine
"The Lord of the Dark Face"	April – May 1929	The Strand Magazine
"The Death Voyage"	October 1929	The Strand Magazine

Novels

A Study in Scarlet (1887)
Micah Clarke (1889)
The Mystery of Cloomber (1889)
The Sign of the Four (1890)
The Firm of Girdlestone (1890)
The White Company (1891)
The Doings of Raffles Haw (1891)
The Great Shadow (1892)
The Refugees (1893)
The Parasite (1894)
The Stark Munro Letters (1895)
Rodney Stone (1896)
Uncle Bernac (1897)
The Tragedy of the Korosko (1898)
A Duet, with an Occasional Chorus (1899)
The Hound of the Baskervilles (1902)
Sir Nigel (1906)
The Lost World (1912)
The Poison Belt (1913)
The Valley of Fear (1915)
The Land of Mist (1926)
The Maracot Deep (1929) Novel with three short stories

Short Story Collections

Mysteries and Adventures (1890)
The Captain of the Polestar and Other Tales (1890)
The Adventures of Sherlock Holmes (1892)
The Gully of Bluemansdyke (1893)
The Memoirs of Sherlock Holmes (1894)

Round the Red Lamp: Being Facts and Fancies of Medical Life (1894)
The Exploits of Brigadier Gerard (1896)
The Green Flag and Other Stories of War and Sport (1900)
The Adventures of Gerard (1903)
The Return of Sherlock Holmes (1905)
Round the Fire Stories (1908)
The Last Galley (1911)
His Last Bow (1917)
Danger! and Other Stories (1918)
Three of Them (1923)
The Case-Book of Sherlock Holmes (1927)

Stage works of Doyle
Jane Annie; or, The Good Conduct Prize (1893) Libretto to operetta, with J.M. Barrie; music by Ernest Ford
Foreign Policy (1893) Based on A Question of Diplomacy
The Story of Waterloo (1894) A one-act play written for Sir Henry Irving
Brothers (1899) Based on novel Halves by James Payn
Sherlock Holmes (1899) with William Gillette
A Duet (1902)
Brigadier Gerard (1906)
The Fires of Fate (1909)
The House of Temperley (1910)
A Pot of Caviare (1910)
The Speckled Band (1910)
The Crown Diamond (1921)
It's Time Something Happened (1925)
Exile: A Drama of Christmas Eve (1925)
The Journey

Poetry
Songs of Action (1898)
Songs of the Road (1911)
The Guards Came Through, and Other Poems (1919)
The Poems of Arthur Conan Doyle: Collected Edition (1922)

Non Fiction
The Great Boer War (1900)
The War in South Africa – Its Cause and Conduct (1902)
Through the Magic Door (1907)
The Crime of the Congo (1909)
The Case of Oscar Slater (1912)
The German War: Some Sidelights and Reflections (1914)
A Visit to Three Fronts (1916)
The British Campaign in France and Flanders1916–20
Memories and Adventures (1924)

Spiritualist and Paranormal Books
The New Revelation (1918)
The Vital Message (1919)
Verbatim Report of a Public Debate on 'The Truth of Spiritualism' between Sir Arthur Conan Doyle and Joseph McCabe (1920)
The Wanderings of a Spiritualist (1921)
The Coming of the Fairies (1922)

The Case for Spirit Photography (1922)
Our American Adventure (1923)
Our Second American Adventure (1924)
The Spiritualist's Reader (1924)
The History of Spiritualism (1926)
Phineas Speaks (1927)
Our African Winter (1929)
The Edge of the Unknown (1930)

Pamphlets

A Full Report of a Lecture on Spiritualism Delivered by Sir Arthur Conan Doyle at the Connaught Hall, Worthing on Friday July 11th 1919 (1919) 11 pages
Our reply to the Cleric: Sir Arthur Conan Doyle's Lecture in Leicester, October 19th 1919 (1920) 16 pages
Spiritualism and Rationalism (1920) 32 pages
The Early Christian Church and Modern Spiritualism (1925) 12 pages
Psychic Experiences (1925) 12 pages
A Word of Warning (1928) 19 pages
What Does Spiritualism Actually Teach and Stand For? (1928) 16 pages
The Roman Catholic Church: A Rejoinder (1929) 72 pages
An Open Letter to Those of My Generation (1929) 12 pages
The New Revelation (1997) 32 pages

www.ingramcontent.com/pod-product-compliance
Lightning Source LLC
Chambersburg PA
CBHW060143050426
42448CB00010B/2278